Internal Controls in Accounts Payable

Mary S. Schaeffer

ISBN: 0615997023
ISBN-13: 978- 0615997025

TABLE OF CONTENTS

Introduction

To some, accounts payable may seem like an innocuous function, necessary but not really requiring much attention, resources or direction. Taking this view is unfortunate because the end result can be a serious negative impact on the bottom line. Even those who recognize the folly of this view don't always devote the attention needed to the payment process.

Too often executives will say something like, "I'm a big picture person" or "I set policy and let my staff take care of the rest." But at the end of the day, the devil in the procure-to-pay process is in the details. Regrettably not everyone is willing to roll up their sleeves and get involved in the nitty-gritty. And, it's in the little details where fraud, duplicate pays and improper payments slip through.

If the excesses of the late nineties demonstrated anything it was that wild uncontrolled spending and "investing," lack of controls and a complete disregard for sturdy financial practices could result in the downfall of what would have otherwise been a very profitable enterprise.

Without a doubt, strong internal controls can make a big difference. They prevent both the outsider (often operating in another country) as well as the devious insider (yes, a very few employees will steal from their employers) from getting their hands on your organization's assets. The goal of this work is to identify the controls that every organization should have within their accounts payable function.

It begins with a discussion of why internal controls are so

important. Once professionals understand all the implications, they are more apt to take the issue seriously. We then continue with a discussion of the internal controls theory and then how to put it into practice in your accounts payable process.

It would be hard to discuss internal controls without touching on the primary outcome of the lack of controls: fraud. So, we do discuss the issue in its own chapter as well as throughout various other sections, where applicable. The issue of duplicate payments is also addressed. This is particularly important because so few vendors return duplicate payments. It is up to the paying company to realize they have paid twice and then to recover that money. They can either handle this process themselves or hire a third party to do so. In either event, it is costly. The expense can be avoided completely by tightening controls so duplicate payments don't slip through, in the first place.

I've been following accounts payable issues for a number of years and one of the things that always surprises me is the number of odd places where internal controls breakdown. In fact, I do a one-hour talk on often over-looked internal control breakdowns in accounts payable. That talk has been converted to a chapter in this work.

After reviewing the relevant issues on internal controls, the work then walks through the process, beginning with the purchase order. At each phase of the procure-to-pay process, appropriate internal controls are identified. Invoice processing, payments made by checks, payments made by purchase cards, payments made electronically and master vendor file are all investigated from a control standpoint.

While it may seem to some that we should be about finished at this point, there are still more internal control issues to be investigated, if we want to do a complete job when it comes to your organization's payment function. Before closing internal controls in your expense reimbursement and avoiding bribing foreign government officials are covered. We also take a look at controls that should be put in place to cover the personal devices (smartphones and tablets) many employees are starting to use at work. These can present control issues.

Finally, we take a look at a few internal control topics (dumpster diving, petty cash boxes, sharing of passwords, what to do when an employee leaves etc.) that didn't fit elsewhere. We close with a look at the accounts payable policy and procedures manual and how it can help tighten controls.

Making sure you have appropriate internal controls in your accounts payable function may be the most important issue you can address to protect your organization's profitability. Don't dismiss the issue as trivial or not worthy of your attention.

Mary S. Schaeffer

Internal controls are a framework, of policies, procedures, analysis and strategies put in place by the organization to prevent fraud, ensure the veracity and reliability of financial and accounting information and to protect the organization's financial assets, including but not limited to its cash flow.

Chapter 1: Why Internal Controls Matter

Let's face it; if you've worked in accounts payable or another accounting area for more than a few weeks you understand the importance of strong internal controls. Yet, more than a few organizations allow their controls to weaken. The possible problems related to flawed internal controls fall into the following areas:

- Fraud
- Duplicate Payments
- Regulatory Non-Compliance
- Other Issues

Let's examine the potential fallout from each of these issues.

Fraud

This is the obstacle most think of when the matter of weak controls is raised. Without a doubt weak internal controls make it easier for anyone to perpetrate a fraud. It is important to realize that fraud is not only a risk from outsiders, you also have internal issues.

Unfortunately, the group of people who knows best where your control weaknesses are, are your employees. While most would never dream of taking advantage of that knowledge, a few would. Not only do they know where the potential loopholes are they know how to exploit them.

Weakened internal controls that lead to process problems have another unintended ramification. More than a few frauds start with an honest mistake. Maybe a vendor sent a second invoice because you paid a discrepant invoice late. And if your processes aren't perfect, a second payment was made. This causes a light to go off at the less-than-scrupulous vendor who realizes your processes aren't what they should be. So, the supplier in question starts sending second and sometimes third invoices regularly.

Another common example of an honest mistake leading to an ongoing fraud is the employee who mistakenly submits the same expense on two different expense reports. When he or she realizes that the expense was paid twice, a light goes off. They quickly figure out they can (and they subsequently do) submit the same expense multiple times.

Duplicate Payments

The prevention of both duplicate payments and fraud go hand in hand. What you do to stop one will almost always do double duty. So, it should be no surprise to readers to learn that weak internal controls are also likely to lead to duplicate payments.

As most readers are aware, and unfortunately few outside the accounts payable/accounting function realize, few vendors return those excess payments. They deposit them and leave them for investigation at a later point. When that occurs, some issue credit memos for the duplicate payment.

This is where the matter gets a little tricky. Even if the vendor issued the credit memo, accounts payable may or may not get it. This is for a variety of reasons, and is one of the numerous reasons why AP Now strongly recommends regular statement audits looking for open vendor credits.

But let's say the vendor does issue the credit memo and it makes it to your accounts payable department. In most of these cases the credit memo is used appropriately. But in a few cases processors don't recognize the credit memo and thinking it is an invoice, they pay it. That's why it is crucial all processers are trained to recognize credit memos and know how to handle them.

The remaining issue when discussing duplicate payments is what happens to those open credits if the customer doesn't claim them. In theory, after a few years, they should be turned over to the states as unclaimed property. This only happens in a small fraction of the cases. In reality, the professional charged with the accounts receivable function at your vendor will use them to cover accrued but unpaid late fees, unearned early payment discounts taken, or disputed invoices. "But wait," you say, "we have a policy of not paying those things."

That may very well be the case, but you won't be consulted on the matter. It will just happen and your open credits will vanish into thin air. That's another reason why frequent statement audits are strongly recommended.

Regulatory Non-compliance

For many, the mention of internal controls triggers thoughts of the Sarbanes-Oxley (S-Ox) Act and the requirement for the certification of strong internal controls. And there's good reason for that. But it should not be the only regulatory concern when it comes to internal controls.

When controls are weak not only is the required certification for S-Ox in jeopardy, but so is the ability to conform to a whole slew of other regulatory issues. If controls are tight and needed information recorded, the ability to conform to the laws related to issues like 1099 reporting, accrual of use tax, independent contractor classification, and unclaimed property requirements will be in jeopardy.

This hidden cost of less-than-ideal internal controls should not be underestimated. The expense and aggravation associated with an audit of any of the issues mentioned above can be quite high.

As you can probably figure out, all the issues in all three categories affect the productivity of the accounts payable function and the profitability of the organization as a whole in a negative way. Don't overlook any of them when evaluating the cost of weak controls across your procure-to-pay process.

Other Reasons

From time to time, most people who work in accounts payable run into a smart-aleck who demands to know "what's the big deal about accounts payable?" These folks think that an effective accounts payable process is one where someone sits at a desk and simply writes checks for any invoice that crosses their desk. As those who work in the function know only too well, this practice would be a recipe for disaster. Here's a look at what could go wrong should an organization be foolish enough to follow such a practice.

- **Reason #10**: Let's get the obvious reason out of the way. Sarbanes-Oxley is a serious consideration for all public companies, as well as a good number of private ones. Some lenders require Sarbanes-Oxley-like compliance from the companies they lend money to.

- **Reason #9**: Some public companies require their suppliers to be Sarbanes-Oxley compliant. They don't want to be dragged through the mud when one of their key suppliers ends up in trouble that could have been easily avoided, if they had stronger internal controls.

- **Reason #8**: As long as the organization was not concerned about the bottom line (and virtually all are!) ignoring best practices would be fine. For duplicate invoices and other excess expenses comes right off the bottom line impacting the profitability of the organization in a negative manner.

- **Reason #7**: When best practices are not followed, payments are typically delayed. This does not sit well with vendors. Typically, when payments are delayed, vendors have a difficult time getting a straight answer as to when they can expect their payments. None of this is conducive to strong relations and hence vendor relations tend to be damaged.

- **Reason #6**: While best practices result in an efficient accounts payable function, the reverse is true when best practices are ignored. The end result is that additional staff will be needed to handle the same amount of work.

- **Reason #5**: It will come as no surprise to those reading this to learn that inefficient processes lead to increased expense for the accounts payable function. This may come in the form of extra staff, lost early payment discounts or late fees.

- **Reason #4:** Strong internal controls translate into a more efficient accounts payable process. This usually means the function does not inadvertently impact the bottom line in a negative manner.

- **Reason #3**: Often times, not employing best practices results in inaccurate information which trickles down to the financial statements resulting in inaccurate financial statements. This is a worst case scenario and one that every organization should strive to avoid. It can also mean being singled out by auditors (internal or external) for financial statement issues. This is not an area where most accounts payable departments have any interest in being mentioned and most strive to avoid it.

- **Reason #2**: Inaccurate financial statements and financial reporting can lead to trouble for executives relying on faulty financial information for business decisions. Use of best practices in the accounts payable arena can lead to improved forecasting, especially when it comes to cash flow.

- **Reason #1**: If everything discussed so far has not been enough to convince you that best practices are a necessity, consider the following. By not using best practices across the entire accounts payable function you could be courting trouble with the IRS and state taxing authorities. All are looking for funds to bolster their sagging coffers. For example, many believe that under reporting of income by independent contractors and other self-employed individuals are largely responsible for the tax gap. The attention on this issue is focused on the corporate world with regards to the sometimes lackadaisical practices when it comes to 1099 reporting by some organizations.

Along the same lines, many believe that only one-third of all organizations that should be reporting and remitting unclaimed property are actually doing so. The result is that many organizations are wide open for trouble in this regards. And, you don't have to go far to find a story bewailing online sales on the Internet and its impact on the states collection of sales and use tax.

Given these issues and others, it is imperative that all organizations look at their accounts payable function and employ as many best practices as they can integrate across the entire cycle.

Chapter 2: The Basics of Internal Controls: The Theory

Internal controls across the accounts payable function are critical for those looking to avoid inefficient operations, excessive payments and fraud. Let's look at some of the issues that impact controls. In this section we take a look at the following issues:

- Segregation of duties
- Background checks
- Poor practices that signal weak internal controls
- Related internal control practices

Segregation of Duties

In order to perpetrate a fraud through accounts payable it is frequently necessary to have access to more than one function. For example, a person would have to have access to the check stock and the facsimile signer. Thus one of the easiest ways to prevent fraud is to assign responsibilities in such a manner to minimize this risk.

Alternatively, close scrutiny on a regular basis of any person with multiple conflicting responsibilities is recommended. Companies sometimes get lulled into a false sense of security because the particular employee with multiple conflicting responsibilities has been with them a long time. This is a mistake as most frauds are committed by long-time trusted employees.

Depending on the size of the department, it may be necessary to work with another group to achieve a full segregation of duties. Under these circumstances there are two options as follows:

1) Most typically, certain tasks have to go elsewhere; or

2) Additional checks are built into the process to ensure there's no fraud.

What Gets Moved

The most common task that ends up leaving accounts payable is responsibility for the master vendor file. If the purchasing staff isn't sufficiently large enough either, then master vendor file sometimes ends up in another area in accounting. While it's nice to have it in accounts payable, that is not the critical issue.

What is key is that it is handled in a unit that can 1) provide the appropriate segregation of duties and 2) will take the task seriously and handle it in a timely manner.

The other task that sometimes gets moved out of accounts payable is that thankless job of getting manual signature put on checks, if that is required. This is a task that most accounts payable departments are only too happy to have someone else take on.

Unclaimed property reporting, check printing, issuance of 1099s are other tasks that also get moved, if needed.

The Future

Regrettably, as long as everyone isn't 100% honest in the workplace, segregation of duties will be an issue all are forced to deal with on a regular basis. This could become a challenge as companies automate their accounts payable function, start making electronic payments in serious numbers and continue to implement process improvements that make the entire accounts payable function more efficient. These very positive actions will result in smaller more proficient staffs.

And therein lies the problem. While smaller more efficient staffs are something just about every organization desires the end result may cause a segregation of duties problem. This is not to say that readers shouldn't try to make process improvements. They should. But it also means they need to be cognizant of the fact that there could be segregation of duties issues down the road. It wouldn't hurt to start thinking now of how you'd like to solve those dilemmas.

The accounts payable world is definitely evolving and with those changes comes challenging and interesting new conundrums.

Reasonable Hiring and Background Checks

Because the employees in accounts payable are sometimes viewed as clerks not much consideration goes into the hiring or background checking process. This can be a huge mistake as the employees in the department regularly come in contact with or have access to the organization's lifeblood – its money.

Should a fraud occur on your watch and it is perpetrated by someone on the accounts payable staff, the manager should be able to demonstrate that reasonable care was exercised in hiring that person. This is not to say that reference checks will necessarily uncover a potential thief but they will cover the bases for the manager who made the unfortunate decision to hire the individual. Often just a few phone calls will uncover enough information to raise a red flag.

The phone calls may not uncover a potential thief, even if the person providing the reference has knowledge of prior wrong doings. The reason for this is that many companies refuse to provide references only verifying that the individual had worked for them for a particular period. Fear of lawsuits due to unfavorable references has forced many to set a corporate policy of just providing the equivalent of name, rank, and serial number. This is unfortunate because often employees who deserve sterling references are hung out to dry because of these policies.

Strong Controls throughout the Accounts Payable Process

Two problems that have plagued accounts payable departments everywhere are fraud and duplicate payments. The two are often mentioned in the same breath because the controls to prevent the latter also help with the former. Although this is starting to change, many organizations often looked at their accounts payable operations as a bunch of clerks who pay the bills – and how hard can that be? The answer is not too hard if you don't care about:

- Timely payments and vendor relations
- Check fraud
- Duplicate payments
- State audits for unclaimed property
- State sales and use tax audits
- B-Notices for incorrect 1099s
- Penalties for incorrect 1099 reporting
- Payment of independent contractors' taxes because of failure to obtain proper 1099 information
- Employee phony invoicing schemes
- Censure by the IRS for inappropriate reporting of non-resident alien income
- Inaccurate or incomplete accruals
- Inaccurate financial statements
- Failure of a Sarbanes-Oxley audit

These are just a few of the areas that a company can run into trouble with if proper policies and controls are not fully integrated into an organization's accounts payable function.

Establish the appropriate controls throughout the function even if it means that the comfortable routines of a few people will be disturbed. In the long run it will benefit your organization.

Eliminate Really Bad Accounts Payable Practices

More organizations than you would suspect employ what are generally considered really bad practices in some parts of their process. Many of these are inherited practices (we always did it that way) and others are a result of corporate culture (boys will be boys). Whatever the reason, Sarbanes-Oxley has shone its light on these dirty little secrets and at least some of the organizations that tolerated these practices are finally letting go of them. Before listing them, we have to salute the accounts payable professionals who seized the opportunity presented by Sarbanes-Oxley and use the Act as ammunition to get rid of the practices. Here are just a few of them:

- Petty cash box
- Not enforcing the T&E policy equitably across the board
- Questionable Travel and Entertainment reimbursement practices
- Not using positive pay
- Not using a duplicate payment audit firm because the company "never" makes duplicate payments (since these firms almost always work on a contingency basis, why not verify that claim)
- Allowing frequent rush checks to cover employee sloppiness
- Not mandating the use of a corporate T&E card
- Not requiring a W-9 before a payment is made to a vendor
- Ignoring the unclaimed property laws

You can probably identify more in your own organization. Very few groups are immune from employing one or two bad practices somewhere across their financial spectrum. Once you've identified them, try and root them out. If you need help, both your internal and external auditors are likely to be in your corner so get their support.

Related Internal Control Concepts

Audit Trails

Now more than ever it is crucial that a trail – be it paper or electronic – be established and easily verifiable. Timely documentation and a record retention policy that assures a clear audit trail are two good first steps toward complying with Sarbanes-Oxley as well as proof to state and federal auditors should your organization come under scrutiny by the authorities for not complying with one of their programs.

A verifiable audit trail ties into the concept of strong internal controls. Review your processes to ensure that the audit trail is there. Some companies find that they need to review their indexing procedures to get an acceptable audit trail.

Monitoring Reports

Establishing effective controls, unfortunately, is not a one-shot project; it is an ongoing process. To ensure that the controls remain effective and function appropriately they need to be reviewed on a periodic basis. Additionally, and equally important, reports need to be designed to ensure that the controls function as they should. They are also part of the control process. These reports can be best designed by figuring out where the potential weaknesses are in the process.

For example, one of the most common ways for an employee to commit check fraud is for the employee to simply change the mailing address of a vendor in the master vendor file. Then, once the check has been mailed, the employee with access to the master vendor file goes back into the system and changes the address back to the correct address. It often takes months for it to come to light that the check went to the wrong vendor and an even longer time to track down where the check did go. If the employee is smart, they will have covered their tracks by that time.

How can you uncover this little scheme? A report of all changes to the master vendor file should be run each week (or month) and the report reviewed by someone at a fairly senior level not related to the process. By looking at all the changes this little scheme would be uncovered. The problem with this approach is that few executives at senior levels want to wade through the minutia of the changes made to the master vendor file.

Review your own processes and find the applicable weak spots and then design your own reports. Depending on your processes you may need a few or many such reports. For example, if inactive vendors are infrequently (or heaven forbid, never) deactivated in the master vendor file, you'll need to review any activity in formerly inactive accounts. A shrewd employee might use one of these accounts, along with some address changes to the master vendor file, to submit a phony invoice, get it approved, and then maneuver your organization's money into his or her bank account. By the way, if management is dragging its heels at deactivating inactive vendors, you might point this scheme out to them.

Training

In many organizations the accounts payable group gets the short shrift when it comes to continuing education. This is unfortunate and to be perfectly honest, not really fair. On one hand, the organization relies on its accounts payable staff to:

- Keep the organization compliant with all regulatory issues
- Keep up to date on each year's changes to the 1099 filing requirements
- Know what's going on with regard to unclaimed property legislation
- Be able to recommend and employ the best practices for the payables process including all sorts of technological advances
- Help prevent check fraud by implementing the latest controls available as well as knowing about all regulatory changes
- Establish routines that minimize duplicate payments

- Integrate the sales and use tax calculations from as many as 10,000 taxing authorities into their daily routines
- Spot phony invoices when they are submitted
- Tactfully deal with belligerent and often uncooperative vendors
- Skillfully handle angry employees who need T&E reimbursements despite the fact that their boss has still not approved their expense report

For a variety of reasons, many organizations do not allocate anything for training the hard working accounts payable professionals who staff their organizations. This is a crime. Currently there are several organizations that provide training in all these areas. They offer onsite conferences where your professional staff can network with other professionals and learn from the best.

For organizations that do not wish to send their staff a distance, there are several groups that offer one-day local seminars.

And, if the staff can't leave the office, the Internet now brings the learning right into your office. And, of course, there are also books, online learning alternatives and newsletters to help keep your staff up-to-date.

Chapter 3: The Basics of Internal Controls: In Practice

Strong internal controls are something that virtually every well-run organization aspires to. But, when the rubber hits the road and it's time to implement, those controls are often not as easy to live with.

In this section we investigate:

- Problems created by inappropriate segregation of duties
- Common control conflicts
- Practices that make AP more efficient and may tighten controls at the same time

Problems Created by Inappropriate Segregation of Duties

One of the principles related to strong internal controls is the appropriate segregation or separation of duties. When it comes to the procure-to-pay cycle, this means that no one person should have the ability to perform more than one piece of the transaction. By restricting this access it becomes more difficult for an employee to defraud the organization. Typically, collusion makes a fraud easier to commit. With the same person handling two or more legs of a transaction, the collusion is a done deal.

Segregation of Duties Problems

One of the more basic ways that fraud occurs in any organization is when the appropriate checks and balances are not in place. In accounts payable this is an important component of strong internal controls. There are certain functions that need to be segregated. For example, a person who can enter an invoice for payment should not also be able to set up a new vendor in the master vendor file or make changes to that file.

As a general rule of thumb, no employee, regardless of title or rank, should be able to handle two functions such that they would be in a position to defraud the organization through a manipulation of those responsibilities. So for example, authorized check signers should not be able to issue and/or print checks. The section below on Common Conflicts contains a list of responsibilities that might be constructed as inappropriate segregation of duties.

While a lot of this may seem like common sense, it can cause problems in small departments. In some instances it will not be possible to segregate duties appropriately without involving employees from another department. And, that is what should be considered.

Even departments that can adequately segregate duties sometimes run into trouble when employees take vacation or are unexpectedly absent. Thus, it is a good idea to perhaps work with another group in smaller organizations.

And, finally, even where it appears there is adequate staff to segregate duties, there can be problems. If there is just enough staff problems can arise when:

- There is a natural disaster
- The backup staff is out in combination with a planned absence
- One or more employees leave the company
- Planned staff reductions (because management rarely thinks about the effects on the segregation of duties when reductions are mandated)

Dissecting the Procure-to-Pay Process

Typically there are three distinct departments involved in the procure-to-pay operation of any company. They are the purchasing department, the receiving department and the accounts payable department. Rarely do the responsibilities handled in one department overlap into a second. However, organizations with smaller accounts payable or purchasing functions may sometimes find themselves stretched to assign tasks in such a way that there are no segregation of duties issues.

Before we look at some of the potential problems that might arise if duties aren't separated appropriately, let's take a look at the different steps along the procure-to-pay trail. Most companies have different parties handling each of the following:

1. Ordering goods
2. Approving purchases
3. Receiving ordered materials
4. Approving invoices for payment
5. Processing invoices
6. Handling preprinted check stock
7. Signing checks/releasing ACH payments
8. Setting up vendors/change vendor information in the Master Vendor File
9. Handling Unclaimed Property reporting
10. Reviewing and reconciling financial records including bank recs

Common Control Conflicts

When two or more legs of the transaction are handled by the same person, there can be a problem. Now, for example, if an organization had one individual ordering goods and doing the unclaimed property reporting, there wouldn't be much of an issue. The problem is the skillset needed to do those two tasks are so disparate that no organization would have the same person performing them. The problem occurs with tasks that are in the same chain. Let's take a look at what can go wrong when certain responsibilities are handled by the same individual.

Potential Conflict #1: If the same person orders goods and then approves the purchases, there is no control and no checks and balances. Of course, the person who ordered the goods might have to review the purchase to ensure that what is on the invoice is what was ordered and not something entirely different.

Potential Conflict #2: If the same individual orders and receives purchases, there is no control over whether the goods were actually ordered in the first place. All an employee who wanted to defraud the company would have to do would be to send an invoice and claim it had been received. Alternatively, low-quality goods could be ordered while the invoice might reflect the price of much higher priced materials.

Potential Conflict #3: If the same person received goods and approved invoices for payment there would be no controls over the pricing or quality.

Potential Conflict #4: If the same individual approved purchases and set up vendors in master vendor file, it would be very easy to set up a phony vendor and submit a fraudulent invoice for goods that do not go through the companies receiving channel.

Potential conflict: #5: If the same individual could approve invoices and process invoices, there would be no controls in place to ensure the invoice was legitimate to start with. The crook would submit and approve a phony invoice and then the processor would run it through allegedly verifying it.

Potential conflict #6: B allowing the same person to process invoices and set up vendors in the master vendor file you open the door to someone setting up a phony vendor in the master vendor file and then processing an invoice against it as though it had been approved by a purchaser.

Potential conflict #7: Permitting one person to both process invoices and sign checks or release ACH payments, you are removing the checks and balances put in place to prevent an employee from processing a phony invoice or sending it to the wrong address.

Potential conflict #8: If one individual can approve invoices and set up vendors in the master vendor file, they can set up a phony vendor, submit a phony invoice and then approve it for payment. When the approved invoice shows up in accounts payable, the processor won't really know they are handling a fraudulent invoice and it will fly through your process – especially if it is for a non-PO item.

Potential conflict #9: if the same person handles preprinted check stock and signed checks, they are effectively set up with a blank company check.

Potential conflict #10: If the same person reconciles the bank account statements and handle unclaimed property reporting, they will know which checks haven't cleared. This will enable them to easily adjust the records so when the unclaimed property is turned over to the state, it is reported in their name instead of the rightful owner's name. The company's records will balance and unless the rightful owner comes forward (unlikely) the employee will claim the money that did not belong to them and no one will be the wiser.

Concluding Thoughts

Inappropriate segregation of duties is one sign of weak internal controls. We've uncovered ten of them above but you can probably come up with a lot more. Now, some organizations just don't have enough people working in accounts payable and purchasing to implement all the separations discussed above. They have two options.

1) Enlist employees in other departments to handle some of the responsibilities discussed. It is not uncommon to find master vendor file, bank reconciliations and/or unclaimed property handled in another department so the appropriate segregation of duties is maintained.

2) If help is not available from other departments, it is sometimes necessary to add additional steps in the process to make up for the weakened controls. This might be the president or CFO reviewing all checks before they are released in a smaller company.

The important issue is that an organization recognizes where there potential weaknesses are and create additional reviews around them.

Practices that Make AP More Efficient and May Tighten Controls in the Process

You've heard the old adage, work smarter not harder. Sometimes we've been doing things a certain way for so long in accounts payable, it never occurs to us to try another approach. That's where the smarter issue comes in. Sure, it's possible to improve productivity if you spend a lot of money, but that's not what we're talking about. Let's take a look at five practices that would make any accounts payable function run a little more efficiently—and won't require special budget allocations to do so.

1. Start accepting invoices both by e-mail and fax. For many years, companies refused to do this because they were concerned about duplicate payments. But now, we know that it is possible to have original looking documents that are actually copies so not paying from a copy does not provide the protection it once did. By accepting invoices by email and fax you speed up the mail time making it easier to earn early payment discounts. What's more, if you are scanning invoices, an emailed invoice removes the need to scan.

2. Get rid of petty cash boxes, if you still have them. Anecdotal evidence suggests that approximately one-quarter of all organizations still have petty cash boxes. They are huge time wasters, are rarely in balance, and may tempt employees with financial issues. By eliminating petty cash boxes you will make the accounts payable function more efficient and you'll strengthen internal controls. And as an added benefit, your staff will probably be thrilled not having to deal with the sometimes questionable reimbursement requests.

3. Return invoices addressed inappropriately/addressed to no one to the vendor with a polite letter explaining that in order to process invoices efficiently it is imperative that every invoice contain the name of the requisitioner or a purchase order number. Without one of these vital pieces of information, your staff will waste time trying to figure out who ordered the item. You'll also eliminate those fraudulent invoices sent by crooks hoping to entice you to pay.

4. Develop and use strong coding standards for invoices and data entry in the master vendor file. Put it in writing and insist everyone use it. This simple approach will eliminate a good portion of potential duplicate payments. Don't assume everyone would use the same abbreviations as you would. They won't. And, by putting it in writing and giving a copy to every processor, they can refer to it if they have any questions.

5. Eliminate as many paper checks as you can. This can be done by moving small dollar items to p-cards and trying to pay as many vendors as possible using ACH. Paper checks are incredibly inefficient; they require a lot of manual handling, get lost in the mail and are expensive, to boot. On the other hand, electronic payments require no manual handling, are less expensive than paper

checks and have very few or no unclaimed property issues.

6. Don't play favorites with employees from other departments (or for that matter from your own). Don't make exceptions against policy based on how much you like a person. For example, if you always do Rush checks for Jane in accounting, other employees will expect similar treatment. If you don't extend them the same courtesy there's bound to be a lot of complaining and grumbling and accounts payable's image will take a hit. What's more, eventually other groups will figure out who your favorites are and those people will be recruited to come down and ask for exceptions for the rest of their department. Often, when accounts payable plays favorites, it is thought that no one knows. But, like all other gossip in an organization, it spreads faster than anyone might imagine.

7. Don't entertain special requests from vendors to pay them faster than the payment terms agreed to in their contracts. More than occasionally, a vendor will call and ask/demand to be paid more quickly than agree upon terms. Sometimes they'll claim someone in purchasing promised this. Other times, especially when they have gotten to know the processor handling their account well, they'll simply ask for a special favor trying to convince the processor to enter an early due date. While you want your processors to have good relations with your vendors, these relations need to be arm's length and not result in inappropriate actions. This is the first step down that slippery path of fraud due to collusion. While a processor putting something in for payment earlier than it should be paid is not a guarantee that fraud will occur in the future, it is a poor practice and should not be tolerated. Preventing this type of familiarity is another reason for regularly rotating processors.

As you can see, none of the above recommendations require budget allocations. All can be implemented without spending any money. Okay, the not accepting invoices without the name of the requisitioner or a purchase order number does require a postage stamp and an envelope. But you can use a form letter and you don't need budget approval for postage stamps.

These are just a few examples of strategies any organization can implement in their accounts payable department to make it a little more efficient. And, we're certain, if you put your mind to it, you can identify a handful of other practices that will improve departmental productivity without incurring a huge expense.

Chapter 4: Fraud Prevention Controls and Practices

Rarely does a fraud occur in the corporate world when it does not signal a serious breakdown in internal controls, that someone was asleep at the switch. Alternatively, it could mean that the controls didn't breakdown, they were so weak to start with that the only surprise is that fraud didn't occur sooner. In this section, we investigate:

- Types of fraud
- Employee fraud prevention
- Vendor fraud
- Check fraud
- Demand draft fraud

Types of Fraud

Thanks to the Association of Certified Fraud Examiners (ACFE), we have some statistics on corporate fraud. The ACFE refers to this type of fraud as occupational fraud. It is also called employee fraud. By providing an overview of what actually goes on in the corporate world, executives will be able to identify potential similar situations in their own organizations.

ACFE's Biannual Report

The ACFE calls its report, the Report to the Nation. It is produced every two years. Cash Misappropriations have always accounted for large number of the frauds studied. These fell into three categories:

1. **Fraudulent Disbursements**, in which the perpetrator causes his organization to disburse funds through some trick or device. Common examples include submitting false invoices or forging company checks.

2. **Skimming**, in which cash is stolen from an organization before it is recorded on the organization's books and records.

3. **Cash Larceny**, in which cash is stolen from an organization after it has been recorded on the organization's books and records

The definitions of the types of fraud used above came directly from the Report.

Fraudulent Disbursements

The type of fraud that is most frequently related to accounts payable is fraudulent disbursements. Approximately three-quarters of frauds in the study involved some form of fraudulent disbursement. It is instructive to know how these schemes were further broken down.

The following information is from the Report.

- **Billing Schemes**, in which a fraudster causes the victim organization to issue a payment by submitting invoices for fictitious goods or services, inflated invoices, or invoices for personal purchases.

- **Check Tampering**, in which the perpetrator converts an organization's funds by forging or altering a check on one of the organization's bank accounts, or steals a check the organization has legitimately issued to another payee.

- **Expense Reimbursement Schemes**, in which an employee makes a claim for reimbursement of fictitious or inflated business expenses.

- **Payroll Schemes**, in which an employee causes the victim organization to issue a payment by making false claims for compensation.
- **Register Disbursement Schemes**, in which an employee makes false entries on a cash register to conceal the fraudulent removal of currency.

Uncovering Fraud

Most companies would like to believe that their own internal processes are strong enough to catch a disbursement fraud before the money went out the door. Unfortunately that is not always the case. In fact, of the frauds that were uncovered after the fact, internal controls were not a key factor in detecting the fraud. And, when it comes to large cases, that is, those over a million dollars, the internal controls fell down on the job big time.

What is truly frustrating is that uncovering these crimes is often a matter of luck, or rather bad luck on the part of the crook. In a typical report, over one-third of all cases were discovered, not because of any grand work on the part company executives but rather because of a tip. When you combine this with the significant number of cases that are discovered by accident, the matter gets more disheartening.

Who Commits Fraud

The traditional response to the question of who commits fraud against their companies was a long-term trusted male employee. This fact comes through every time the ACFE does this study.

Other factors likely to increase a crook's proclivity for fraud include longer tenures with the company and gender, with more frauds committed by males than females.

Dealing with Employee Fraud

What the ACFE data demonstrates is that there is a need for strong internal controls. Here are some things that can be done to make it difficult for those few employees who would actually defraud their employers.

- **Establish an anonymous hotline.** There are two good reasons to do this. First, it is required by Sarbanes-Oxley. But there's an even better reason. In reviewing the data above, an extremely high percent came from Tips. Make it easy and anonymous for employees to come forward.

- **Make sure that you have the appropriate segregation of duties.** While this will not prevent fraud, it will make it more difficult for potential crooks. With proper segregation of duties certain frauds become impossible to commit without collusion. Unfortunately, this just reduces the incidence of these crimes because occasionally, employees do get together to defraud their employers.

- **Insist that employees take their vacation time.** This is often when an ongoing employee fraud comes to light. Be suspicious of the employee who goes several years without ever taking a day off. The following will be hard to do if your firm only offers two weeks of vacation. Some banks require that employees take at least two consecutive weeks off. It is believed that all frauds will be discovered within that timeframe. If it is reasonable to make this a requirement, do so. And, if it is not, consider rotating employees off their normal assignments for cross-training purposes.

- **Put MCC-code limitations on p-cards.** This needs to be done with care and will prevent employees from making certain unauthorized purchases. However, be aware that the MCC code assignment is not perfect and you could end up creating a few problems.

- **Have a thorough investigation process before hiring a new employee.** Check references and verify former employment. While this will not completely prevent fraud, it will help when it comes to filing a claim in case of a loss. By being able to prove that you took reasonable care in your hiring practices you will have less trouble with the insurance company when filing the claim.

These issues all address your internal control structure.

The Ugly Issue: Employee Fraud Prevention

No one likes to admit it but occasionally an employee will steal from their employer. What's even more disheartening is that year after year, the statistics demonstrate that the most likely people to steal from their employers are long term trusted employees. Now before a few of our readers are offended by that allegation, let me point out that the thieves among us are few and far between. The problem is identifying the crook is not easy. They look like every other long term trusted employee. Let's take a look at some tactics every organization should employ to avoid an employee-theft disaster.

The Big Problem

The reason that organizations with strong internal controls are at such high risk is simple. Their employees know where the weaknesses are and know how to exploit them. What's more, some organizations have great segregation of duties controls set up and then they negate the whole thing by giving one or two "trusted employees" access to everything. Often this works fine, but occasionally it does not.

The other misconception that makes it easy for in-house fraudsters is the sense of complacency some organizations have. They think "it would never happen here" or "we're too big or too small." More than one executive has had to eat his or her our-employees-would-never-steal-from-us words.

Overriding Fraud Prevention/Detection Guidelines

Ideally, your goal should be to deter all potential frauds. By this I mean the controls and monitoring you have in place are so stringent that no one even attempts to steal from your organization. The only problem is there is no way to measure frauds that were deterred so you never really know if you were effective on this front.

If you haven't deterred a fraud and someone is bold enough to try, your next goal should be to prevent it. By this we mean, catch the fraud before the money leaves your bank account. And, finally, if the money does get away, you want to have processes in place to identify the fraud and hopefully recover the funds. If you can't recover the funds, at least you can put a stop to the fraud, if it is ongoing. Many employee frauds are continuing.

The following three principal guidelines will help you structure a framework that will serve to both deter and prevent fraud in your organization.

- Establish a strong internal control framework covering all facets of the payment function. This includes purchasing and receiving and of course, travel and entertainment reimbursements.

- Take segregation of duties seriously and make sure one person cannot do more than one part of the purchase-to-pay process. Regularly review the scope of your employees' access to ensure nothing has gone awry.

- Create a Policy of Zero Tolerance when it comes to any type of fraud or abuse. The policy should come from the highest level executive in the organization along with a letter stating the organization intends to abide by it across all spectrums.

What Else

There are a number of other tactics savvy organizations use, although you'd be amazed to discover the number of businesses that ignore these principles. What follows is a look at three simple steps any organization can use to both prevent and detect fraud.

1) Mandatory vacations. Anyone associated with any part of the payment function should be required to take five consecutive days off and someone else should perform their job function. The theory behind this approach is that in five days an ongoing fraud will unravel. Too often we hear staffers complain that their organization won't allow them to take their vacation because everyone is overworked. This is just asking for trouble. Not only has the organization ignored the five-consecutive vacation tactic, there's a good chance they have an unhappy employee.

2) Job Rotation. This strategy is a little harder to implement if you have a smaller department. And, to be blunt, there are certain functions that cannot be rotated. Asking the corporate head of tax to switch positions with the company's top lawyer is just not going to work. However, if you have more than three or four processors, rotating the suppliers they cover every six months or a year is very feasible. This makes collusion more difficult. What's more, you get the added benefit of having more than one person knowledgeable about different accounts. If you do take this step, and we recommend that you do, it is imperative that you have a strict coding standard and the associates handling your invoices all process exactly the same.

3) Surprise Audits. First and foremost, we're talking about surprise audits of the petty cash box, if you still have one. As most professionals may realize, I strongly recommend the elimination of the petty cash box as a best practice. But, assuming you have one, surprise audits are one way to detect and prevent games in that arena. But, that is not the only auditing you should be doing. Periodically, audit your processors to ensure they are sticking to your rigid guidelines for handling invoices.

If You Suspect Fraud

The first thing to remember if you suspect fraud is that you could be wrong. Not everything is as it appears. So, before accusing do a little research and gather your facts. For, if you accuse some and you are wrong, you will never have the trust of that person again. What's more; the organization's relationship with that person will be strained for some time.

The second reason you don't want to accuse someone before you have all the facts is that you may alert them giving them time to either destroy needed evidence or flee. So, if you don't accuse the person, what should you do?

For starters, immediately share your concerns privately with your boss. He or she will probably want to involve HR and do further research. HR may even bring in a fraud expert to help with the matter. Follow the guidance given by HR on this matter. It is something you really should not address on your own.

Employee fraud is something most of us would prefer happened to the other guy. Unfortunately, we cannot afford to take that view. By bulletproofing your processes you will go a long way towards making sure it doesn't happen on your watch. But, if it does, then prepare to act appropriately.

Vendor Fraud

Fraudulent invoices are a serious issue for corporate America. New vendors should be verified. Have a process in place before a vendor is entered into the Master Vendor File. A form should be filled out and a W-9 obtained. The form should have all relevant data about the vendor. Ideally it should be submitted by one person and approved by a second. When it arrives in accounts payable (or wherever the master vendor file function resides) some additional verification should be done.

When verifying the information provided by the vendor, do not use that data. For example, instead of using the phone number on the application (it's just too easy to provide an incorrect number) get on the Internet and find the number. Check out the address as well. Is it the same? If not, is there a good reason? For example, a company may have a "Pay To" address that is actually its lockbox.

The problem of fraudulent invoices for low-dollar items is one that continues to plague organizations everywhere. Crooks know that if they send a small-dollar invoice (say less than $100) many organizations will simply pay it rather than spend time getting it approved and doing a three-way match. In cases where best practices related to the master vendor file are not strictly followed, some processors will even set the company sending the fraudulent invoice up in the master vendor file.

Once a fraudulent invoice has been paid it is likely the vendor will send another and another. Strong internal controls, the employment of best practices and rigid coding guidelines are the best protection against this type of fraud.

Small Dollar Invoice Fraud

If you work in an organization of any size, you are probably bombarded with invoices for copier toner, yellow pages ads, and a variety of other items never ordered by anyone in your organization. Invariably, you will find that these invoices are for common items at highly inflated prices. Sometimes the goods will even be delivered to your organization and they will be of extremely low quality. This of course makes it a little more difficult because when accounts payable goes to do the three-way match, there is a receiving document. Of course, they can never figure out who ordered the goods. Unfortunately, in the case of toner and copier paper, the goods sometimes get mixed in with the company's supplies and used ... and paid for.

The control issue here is to have some sort of a tracking system for identifying who ordered goods when invoices come into accounts payable without a PO number. Some companies take the aggressive step of returning such invoices to the supplier. They have a policy that states that all invoices must either have a valid PO number or the name of the person who ordered the goods. Others take an even harsher stance. They insist on a PO number and demand that the supplier go back to the person who ordered the item and obtain one. While these practices work well in getting rid of fraudulent invoices, they do not make for good vendor relations.

From a practical standpoint it might seem that it would be reasonable to occasionally pay for these goods rather than invest a lot in setting up controls to avoid paying for them. The problem with that philosophy is that once you pay once, you go on the sucker list and will continue to get billed for inferior products not ordered.

W-9

Some accounts payable departments have trouble getting W-9s from their independent contractors. Because of heightened IRS scrutiny and fines for Form 1099 errors, requiring a W-9 from every vendor should be a no-brainer. However, in some cases there still is reluctance on the part of purchasing to ask suppliers for these documents. It is a control issue for three reasons:

1. It is needed in order to correctly report income and the company could be liable for the taxes owed by the contractor if it is not reported correctly

2. You are not in compliance with Sarbanes-Oxley if W-9s (it's the law) are not gotten and 1099s not issued in an appropriate manner.

3. By getting the W-9 and verifying the TIN (tax identification number)/Name match you are confirming that the vendor is a legitimate entity.

Note: While you've confirmed that the vendor is legitimate, it does not mean necessarily that the invoices it sends your firm are legitimate. That should be addressed in your invoice processing standards and procedures.

From a control point, every company should have a No TIN, No

Payment policy. If a vendor refuses to provide the TIN, simply withhold the appropriate taxes and pay it, if management insists. This will not win you any popularity contests but one has to wonder why a vendor would refuse to provide their TIN.

Check Fraud

Check fraud is a huge problem in the United States. Even as more organizations move toward electronic payments, check fraud continues as the type of payment fraud most commonly attempted. If good controls are used along the entire check processing cycle, you will have diminished, but not eliminated the potential for check fraud. To be perfectly honest, it is unlikely that the threat will ever be completely eradicated. It is an ongoing battle. Every time the corporate world comes up with a solution to a particular form of check fraud, the thieves move on and come up with another variation.

From both a protection standpoint and control issue, positive pay is considered to now be an essential tool in the fight against check fraud. While the number of companies using the many varieties of positive pay is growing, there are still a number who have refused to make the move. That is not wise.

Inactive bank accounts should be closed and any remaining check stock destroyed. This is not likely to be a favorite task among your staff. When we say destroyed, we are not talking about just throwing the checks in the garbage. They should be shredded. This is another reason why companies are moving to laser check stock. There is no check stock to shred when accounts are closed.

While there is some fraud associated with electronic payments, it is, at least at this point, much less common than check fraud. Thus, a move to the electronic world can help in this regard.

Segregation of duties should be strictly adhered to when allocating responsibilities for the various functions in the check production cycle. Each person should have their own password and user ID for any systems used. It is considered a weak control to allow employees to share passwords and it will get your organization in trouble during your Sarbanes-Oxley audit.

Six Practices that Enable Internal Check Fraud

Certain sloppy practices, especially when it comes to checks, actually make it easier for employees to commit check fraud. Allowing these practices to continue is effectively enabling the fraudsters who might be lurking in your corridors. And these are all things you can change without spending a cent. So what are these easy-to-fix processes?

Practice #1 Allowing checks to be returned to the person who requested them. Without a doubt, this is the biggest enabler of them all. And, this is a practice than is permitted in many, many organizations. While we concede there are rare occasions when the checks need to be returned, they are few and far between. We recommend that any organization that allows the return of checks develop a form to be included with the check. The form should be filled out by the person requesting the return and it should be signed by a very senior executive. It should contain a place for the person to enter the reason the check must be returned and not mailed. The form works in two ways to deter fraud. First, few employees will want to get it signed unless the check really must be returned. And, second, a crook will think twice (hopefully) about documenting the request if he or she intends to steal the check. Few thieves want to draw attention to themselves.

Practice #2 Permitting Rush or ASAP checks in all but the most urgent circumstances. When the data is analyzed, Rush checks represent a disproportionate share of both fraudulent checks and duplicate payments. The reason is simple. Crocked vendors know if they call an organization's accounts payable department and threaten to put the company on credit hold, the chance of a Rush manual check being issued is high. So that is exactly what they do. Even if the call is legitimate, the chances are a second or third invoice has been issued before the vendor got desperate enough to call and demand a Rush check. Inevitably, the original invoice eventually makes its way into accounts payable and sometimes gets paid. Part of the reason for this is the manual process sometimes results in records not being updated or entered correctly.

Practice #3 Lack of appropriate segregation of duties. Whenever an employee is authorized to perform two tasks that serve as checks and balances to each other, it increases the risk of fraud. So, making someone a check signer and giving them access to check stock or the ability to approve an invoice increases the ease at which they could commit check fraud, if they wanted to. Thus, especially when it comes to an organization's money, appropriate segregation of duties is crucial.

Practice #4 Giving high level executives access to everything. In some ways, this is a subset of the issue discussed above. There are organizations that go out of their way to set up the appropriate segregation of duties and then give either a high level executive or the accounts payable manager access to everything. This completely negates everything else done. When questioned about it, inevitably the response is that the person in question is a trusted employee. Well, guess who commits most internal fraud? Long term trusted employees!

Practice #5 Making all high level executives authorized signers. In some organizations all vice presidents are put on bank accounts as signers, even if they never sign and check signing is not part of their job. As in the discussion above, this can negates the segregation of duties the organization strove to set up.

Practice #6 Poor master vendor file practices. So many organizations ignore their master vendor file not realizing they are providing the perfect hiding place for employees looking for ways to defraud them. This is especially true when the file is never cleansed and vendors not used in over 12 or 14 months deactivated. It is easy to put this task off when other issues are pressing. But, don't; you are only asking for trouble by leaving inactive vendors in the file. Use of strict coding standards also helps. When was the last time your master vendor file was cleansed?

As we said at the beginning, these practices are fixable at virtually every organization – and the fix doesn't cost a red cent. How many of these practices still exist in your organization?

Demand Draft Fraud

This little known payment devise was designed to accommodate legitimate telemarketers who receive authorization from consumers to take money out of the consumer's checking account. This payment alternative is very similar to writing a check – except that it requires no signature. In place of the authorized signature on the check the words "signature not required, your depositor has authorized this payment to payee" or similar wording is used. Since the check processing areas at banks are completely automated, the signature line is virtually never checked.

In the telemarketer example this is a creative payment approach that enables the transaction to proceed smoothly. Demand drafts are also sometimes referred to as remotely created checks. You can see there is potential for check fraud in this arrangement but then any time a check is used for payment, there is also the possibility for abuse. Once the thief has the account number and the name of the account owner, check fraud is merely a matter of conscience, opportunity, and a few dollars for technology.

Concluding Thoughts

Fraud is a serious problem for all organizations. Often, it indicates that internal controls were less than they should be. While Sarbanes-Oxley has made internal controls a key focal point, consideration to the losses that can accrue because of these frauds is a serious consideration. As the numbers from the ACFE demonstrate, successful frauds typically involve such serious amounts of money that the corporate world is well advised to take as many precautions as it can to prevent them.

Chapter 5: Duplicate Payments and Their Relationship with Poor Internal Controls

An unintended side effect of poor internal controls is the increased likelihood of duplicate payments. One of the dirty little secrets in the corporate world is that few duplicate payments are ever returned. That's right; most vendors don't return those payments. Initially they sit on the vendor's books as open credits but eventually many open credits are used by vendors at the end of the quarter or fiscal year to clean up open outstanding disputed invoices, accrued late fees (which you vehemently refuse to pay) and unearned early payment discounts.

As an added bonus, practices put in place to prevent duplicate payments, also tend to tighten controls. In this section, let's take a look at:

- Traditional techniques that work (and those that don't) in preventing duplicate payments
- Check request practices that help avoid duplicate payments and fraud
- Common scenarios that cause duplicate pays & how to stop them

Traditional Prevention: What Works and What Doesn't

As the accounts payable world continues to evolve, some of the tactics used in the past to prevent duplicate and erroneous payments no longer work. Some of the old standbys no longer cut the mustard.

It would be nice if this overpayment problem would go away; it's been with us forever. Alas, that does not seem likely to happen. So, it is imperative that readers regularly review their procedures to make sure that they are not relying on practices that no longer prevent those nasty duplicates from occurring. What follows is a look at practices that no longer do the job as well as a list of those that do.

What Doesn't Work

- Relying on the "our system will not accept duplicate invoice numbers" control. Even if your accounting system has this feature, virtually every processor knows that if they simply add a blank space, a period or a letter to the end of the invoice number, the "new" invoice will be accepted. Unfortunately, many routinely use this tactic to force invoices through.

- Never paying from copies or faxes. While this was a reasonable approach several years ago, advances in technology make it possible to produce numerous "original" invoices. What's more, some suppliers are insisting on emailing or faxing invoices to save on postage. Upon reflection, receiving invoices electronically or by fax gets them into your process sooner. This makes the earning of early payment discounts a bit easier and avoids invoices lost in the mail – both internal and external.

- Relying on the memory of the processor. This is just as bad an idea today as it was years ago, yet many organizations still expect their processors to recognize duplicates. Let's just say this about it: It doesn't work.

What Does Work

- Require full backup for every single Rush check

- Go through the same rigorous three-way match, extinguishing the PO and receiver etc. when issuing a Rush check as you would with an invoice processed for payment through normal channels.

- Eliminate all but the most essential Rush checks. The number of Rush checks issued each week should be in the single digits. If not, review your processes to determine the problem.

- Make sure POs are extinguished when payment is issued.

- Coordinate processes for payment made by checks, p-cards and ACH. Make sure the same rigorous procedures are used regardless of the payment mechanism.

- Have stringent coding standards for data in the master vendor file.

- Regularly deactivate inactive vendors in the master vendor file.

- Have a rigorous coding standard for invoice data entry that is constructed using the same approaches as your master vendor file coding standard.

- Make sure all your processors use the same coding standards and procedures and none develop their own workarounds.

Concluding Thoughts

Once you've done everything you can to eliminate duplicates call in a contingency fee auditor to take a look at your books. Let them look for duplicates. If you are correct and you've done a good job, they'll find very little and you'll owe them even less. But, if a loophole has developed, they could find a significant amount of money that is rightfully yours. Yes, their fee could be higher than you'd like. But, at least you'll recover a good portion of your money and should be able to find the weak link in your processes that allowed the problem in the first place.

The auditors provide a report detailing any weaknesses

they find. You can use it to tighten your processes. It would be nice if vendors would return duplicate and erroneous payments but in reality that happens in only a small fraction of cases. That's why savvy professionals watch their procedures like a hawk and crack down immediately when they identify a weak link.

Check Request Practices to Avoid Duplicate Payments and Fraud

Ahhh...check requests: that ubiquitous form used to request payments for all sorts of things. Theoretically a solution (by making it easy to request a payment when an invoice is missing) in reality it can create numerous headaches for AP, not to mention causing duplicate payments by the boatload. Here's a look at some of the problems surrounding check requests and a few suggestions on avoiding them.

Background

Check requests are used in most organizations to request a payment when an invoice is not available or was never provided. Ideally, there should be backup documentation augmenting the check request and providing details regarding the payment amount, the payee, and the reason for the payment. Since most payments made on check request forms will *not* go through the rigorous three-way match in accounts payable, the documentation supporting the check request is of utmost importance.

The one exception to this is those groups that require a check request for every single payment. This is not a best practice, although some firms with unique industry or regulatory requirements might find it necessary to go this route.

Where Check Requests Cause Problems

Check requests forms are often used to accommodate rush check requests. These are one-time payments made to vendors outside the normal invoice submission process. Typically this happens when a payment is late and the upset vendor threatens to put the organization on credit hold.

Whether the check request form is used for a rush check or simply because the invoice has been misplaced if the proper documentation is not attached the chances for a duplicate payment skyrocket. Ideally the attached documentation should be the original invoice. Of course, if it were available, there might be no need for the check request form.

Without the invoice to perform the three-way match, the purchase order and receiver often remain open on the organization's books. This can blossom into two types of problems. The most obvious is a duplicate payment made when the invoice finally shows up and is paid in accounts payable.

The less obvious issue is what happens to the open receivers and purchase orders when the financial statements are prepared. There is a chance that the states could view open receivers as unclaimed property. In a few instances companies have reported auditors taking this stance with open receivers that have been on the books for a long period of time without a matching payment.

The final problem relates to fraud. Alas, a great number of fraudulent payments, more than we'd like to think, are issued on check requests. How is this possible? The most obvious answer is a crooked employee fills out the check request form and either convinces an authorized signer to sign it or forges the signature himself.

The other way that fraud occurs with a check request form is in response to an irate vendor claiming non-payment. Some vendors have learned if they get on the phone and are generally abusive with the accounts payable staff threatening credit holds, they can sometimes get a harried controller to sign off on a check request form authorizing the payment. In one of the most egregious examples of this type of fraud a vendor pulled this screaming stunt every month for 18 months—getting double payment for each one. With murky documentation attached to each form, it was difficult to find the duplicates until the entire vendor file was pulled and reviewed.

Best Check Request Practices

There are a number of steps any organization should take to make the check request form work as it is intended without introducing the problems discussed above. Begin by requiring documentation for every check request form. If an invoice, or copy of an invoice, is not available, attach a copy of the contract, an e-mail detailing requirements, or whatever is available. Great care should be taken to avoid sending in the form without any supporting documents

In the extreme cases where no documentation is available—and you know that will happen at some point—require an extra signature of a very high-level executive within the organization, perhaps the controller or the CFO. The person making the request should be ready with a *really* good explanation for why the check should be issued without documentation. Requests without documentation should be few and far between. If there are outstanding POs and receivers related to these requests, that information should be included on the form so accounts payable can extinguish them when the payment is made.

If by some miracle, there is an invoice attached to the check request form, perform the normal three-way match extinguishing both the purchase order and the open receiver.

Reducing the Number of Check Request Forms

If you only have a few check request forms each month to process, there is, in all likelihood, little you can do to decrease the number of them. Like rush checks, a small number is an inevitable part of doing business.

If you get more than a few, for several months, track the requests keeping a log noting:

- The requestor;
- The payee;

- The date of the request; and
- The reason for the request.

When you have the data for a few months, take it out and analyze it. Are most of your requests coming from a few requestors? In that case you might want to have some discussions with those involved to determine where the problem lies.

But before you do that, take a look at the vendors receiving the payments. Are a suspiciously high number of these requests going to the same vendor? This could mean one of two things. The less sinister explanation is that there is a problem somewhere in the process that needs to be fixed so the vendor can receive payment through the normal cycle. The more ominous reason is that there is an ongoing fraud.

If you suspect fraud, do not approach the individuals involved. Get all your facts lined up ask your immediate supervisor to review them and if you both agree something is fishy, get HR involved. They will know the correct way to approach this situation. Discretion is crucial in these cases for two reasons. First, you could be wrong and, secondly, if you are correct, you don't want to tip your hand before the experts decide how to approach the matter.

Check request forms are a necessary evil in the accounts payable world. Work hard to implement best practices surrounding them and the troubles they cause will be held to a minimum.

Common Scenarios that Cause Duplicate Pays & How to Stop Them

New improved payment processes can translate, unfortunately, into new ways to make duplicate payments. The same goes for some of the new wonderful ways to process invoices. This is not to say there is anything wrong with these new processes; quite the contrary. It simply means that the professionals who handle payments must be extra careful to insure that when making payments, they take the time to ensure that the appropriate controls are put in place to guard against duplicate payments. New technologies sometimes mean new controls. In this section we'll look at five scenarios that if you are not careful will open the door for duplicate payments.

Background

When the only way that bills got paid was to receive an invoice and issue a check, it was easier to control duplicate payments. Let me make it perfectly clear that I am not saying it was easy to prevent duplicates; that is never the case. But, there were fewer issues to be concerned about. In this new payment world every payment professional needs to be concerned about the following issues:

- Payments not being made twice using two different payment types

- Other professionals outside accounts payable making payments but not necessarily using the same rigid standards used in accounts payable to ensure duplicate payments are not made

- Unscrupulous employees or vendors taking advantage of the increased "opportunities" to hide a duplicate payment and using it to enrich themselves at your organization's expense.

Scenario #1: Credit Card Payments and Invoices

This issue has been with us for a few years and may be the hardest to fix. Certain vendors claim they cannot suppress the printing of invoices and continue to send invoices even though they were paid at the point of purchase with a credit card. For the purpose of this discussion, let's assume this is true. If you suspect it is not, you should investigate whether your organization wants to continue doing business with the vendor. It is recommended that only one type of payment method be used with each vendor. While this works in theory in practice it is not always possible.

Assuming it is not possible to limit payment methodology, there are two steps you can take to guard against paying these vendors twice. First, teach your processors to check invoices closely. Many of the vendors who cannot suppress the printing of the invoice will mark it with a note saying it was paid by credit card. True, many of these notes are in very small print so your processors will have to look closely to find the note.

If this is not sufficient, consider setting up a separate post office box for those vendors who you sometimes (or always) pay with credit cards. Invoices that arrive at this box can be checked against credit card statements to ensure payment is made only once.

Scenario #2: Extinguishing POs and Receivers

With the widespread introduction of ACH payments, responsibility for making payments is expanding outside accounts payable. That's fine, if that works for the organization. However, and this is a big one, it is imperative that whoever makes the payment takes all the steps that might be taken by a professional in accounts payable. This means using the same rigid coding standards and extinguishing both the PO and the receiver.

We have heard numerous stories about these steps not being adhered to – simply because the professionals involved are not aware of them or do not realize their significance. If these items are left open and a second invoice shows up, the odds of it being paid a second time skyrocket. And there is a new issue looming.

Open receivers are the latest target of unclaimed property auditors. This has become a hot issue for some of the big warehouse stores. Some state auditors have taken the stance that open POs represent unclaimed property and the value of them should be remitted to the states. To call this ugly would be an understatement.

Scenario #3: Travel and Entertainment Reimbursement &

Invoices

Occasionally an employee will pay for something with a personal credit card (or cash) and put in for compensation on his or her T&E expense reimbursement report. There is absolutely nothing wrong with this and in fact it is a recommended approach for small dollar items – another way to get those small dollar invoices out of the accounts payable department.

This assumes that the approach truly does get those small dollar invoices out of accounts payable. Occasionally, an employee has been known to put in for reimbursement on the expense report and submit an invoice for payment. Most of the time, this is not an oversight on the part of the employee or the vendor but is fraud. It is very difficult to catch.

Any time this happens, the employee in question's expense reports should be pulled for the last 18 months and reviewed to see if this was an honest mistake or it is part of an ongoing fraud. It is possible that the vendor is the one pulling a fast one so be careful about pointing a finger – but investigate thoroughly.

Scenario #4: Check Request Forms and Invoices

Different organizations rely on check request forms to different levels. Some use them rarely and others rely on them quite frequently. The problem arises when the backup is scanty (or even nonexistent) and is for an invoice. If the invoice is not attached and/or if that information is not keyed into the system, a duplicate payment will invariably be made when that original invoice eventually finds its way into accounts payable – and you know it will.

In fact, research shows that Rush checks (often issued with a check request form) are one of the leading causes of duplicate payments. We realize that check request forms and Rush checks are here to stay. What we recommend is a stringent requirement for backup and that invoice information be keyed at the time the check is issued. Otherwise, prepare for an onslaught of duplicates.

Scenario #5: Printing Electronic Invoices

Are you part of the electronic revolution receiving invoices electronically? Do some of those invoices arrive as attachments to e-mail? If so, make sure your processors are not printing them before processing and then inadvertently processing the printed invoice as well as the electronic one.

If you have very rigid standards for entering invoice numbers and coding standards this should not cause you problems. But even the best processors sometimes let one slip by. One manager we know took the print key off her processors computers to put an end to the printing of invoice information. She was concerned about the loss of productivity so the chance to reduce potential duplicates was just a side benefit.

Closing Thoughts

Clearly as the payment world evolves there will be loopholes that permit duplicate payments, if those using the new methodologies are not careful. By taking the time to set up the right controls and make sure that *all* affected parties adhere to the procedural instructions, you should be able to limit the problem.

Chapter 6: Where Internal Controls Breakdown

Appropriate internal controls cover virtually every facet of an organization's processes. This is especially true of the procure-to-pay chain. Many times there are issues that don't readily pop to mind when thinking about controls. This section focuses on those facets. In this section we look at:

- The overlooked people issue
- The payment process
- AP practices
- Why internal controls sometimes fail and how to prevent those failures

The Internal Controls Breakdown: The Overlooked People Issues

Some of our internal controls breakdowns occur in often-overlooked people issues. They are either tasks we forget to do or ones we dismiss as not being critical. Whether they occur through benign neglect or oversight, every organization needs to take steps to eliminate these potential control breakdowns. In this article we'll take a look at common control failures related to segregation of duties, employee departures and expense reimbursements.

Segregation of Duties

One of the key tenets in a good internal controls program is the appropriate segregation of duties. When it comes to accounts payable, this ensures that no one individual handles or has access to more than one step in the procure-to-pay process.

This makes it more difficult for fraud to slip through without some sort of collusion. Two of the most common times when appropriate segregation of duties are overlooked are 1) when an employee is promoted and 2) the exceptions. Let's take a look to see what can go wrong in both these cases.

While we are strong advocates of promoting from within, AP Now cautions everyone that when it is done care should be taken to ensure that the access the employee had in his or her old position is cut off. So, if you have someone who was processing invoices and promote them to handle the master vendor file, cut off their ability to process invoices right before you give them access to make changes to the master vendor file. This one little step is often forgotten in numerous organizations. And, this is not just a mistake made in accounts payable. Organizations make it across the board in all departments.

The second problem that occurs more frequently than we'd like to admit is when companies make one exception to the segregation of duties assignments. Usually they've done an exceptional job setting up their delegations for segregation of duties and then ruin it by making one big exception, usually for either the accounts payable manager or the controller. Unfortunately, this negates all their good work. They usually have a plausible excuse for this departure, but not one good enough. At the end of the day, the need for appropriate segregation of duties trumps ease of operation and the like.

Departing Employees

Whether the company is dancing the proverbial jig or crying buckets over an employee who is leaving the company, the steps it should take with regard to internal controls are the same. These steps are rarely taken. When someone leaves an organization, you should:

1. Immediately cut off their system access.

2. Get all credit cards back. This includes T&E cards, fuel cards and any corporate procurement cards.

3. Notify the bank immediately and cancel all cards. Remember, just because the employee returned the credit cards, doesn't mean the credit card numbers and expiration dates weren't written down before the cards were turned in.

4. If the departing employee had any signing rights for checks or could approve or initiate wire or ACH transactions, immediately suspend those rights. Call the bank and follow up with a written notification.

5. If you enter your employees in the master vendor file for expense reimbursement purposes don't forget to deactivate them when they leave the company so they can't slip through one last unauthorized expense report.

Expense Reimbursements

The IRS has strict requirements about what's required as documentation of expenditures for accountable plans. So, when it comes to expense reimbursements, it's not only a matter of internal controls, it's also a matter of endangering the organization's accountable plan status. And to be fair, this is also an issue of what the organization feels it should pay for and what the employee should pay for.

The first concern is that of who attended a business event. IRS requires the listing of every attendee at a business event. This information should include not only their name, but their title, name of their organization and business relationship with the organization. Your employees should include this on their expense reimbursement requests. Verifying this is difficult if not impossible, but you can get an idea of how many people attended – if you get the detailed meal receipt. That will show how many main courses were ordered. This is not a perfect control but probably the best you can do. We should also note that not every organization is willing to do this kind of verification although we are seeing a growing number request the detailed meal receipt.

The detailed meal receipt can also be used to verify that no employee has surreptitiously added a gift card when taking a guest out for a meal at the company's expense. One would hope that if the organization required the detailed meal receipt, employees would be smart enough not to include a gift card for themselves.

The last overlooked expense reimbursement issue involves what was really ordered.

When an employee submits an expense report with only the total amount showing, there's no way to tell what actually was ordered. Two examples shared by our readers bring home the point. One involves an employee who frequently put in for business entertainment on a Friday night. When the detailed meal receipt for one particular Friday night was obtained it showed two adult meals and two kiddie meals. This makes one wonder who actually was at that dinner. The second involved what was supposed to be a job discussion. The detailed receipt showed a plate of wings and a dozen beers.

Do all employees play these games? We do not believe so; in fact, we think the number that does is a small minority. However, we have seen an increase in the number of companies requiring the detailed meal receipt and we can only think it is to address issues such as those discussed here. Please remember, that just because you require all receipts or the detailed meal receipts doesn't mean you have to check them all. The purpose of requiring the receipts is to serve as a deterrent to those employees thinking of ordering something they shouldn't. Spot checking of receipts is typically sufficient.

Strong internal controls protect any organization. It is important to make sure yours cover the often over-looked people issues.

Internal Controls Breakdown: The Payment Process

Strong internal controls are the underpinning of a payment process that doesn't leak profits and runs as efficiently as possible. They are a big component in any fraud prevention program and as an added bonus, go a long way in preventing duplicate payments. But occasionally, controls break down. This most typically happens when the process in question is something outside the norm. A company may have great controls for the bulk of its transactions but those one-offs and infrequent transactions can cause control problems if thought is not given to incorporating good processes for those rare occasions. When it comes to payments this can happen in three arenas; wire transfers, payments made outside accounts payable and with recurring payments. Let's take a look at each.

Wire Transfers

Traditionally, wire transfers were made when the payment amount was large and/or the payment was going across borders from one country to another. With the growing use of ACH some of the wire activity has migrated away to the ACH arena. Wire transfers are relatively expensive and often result in same day availability of funds. They are made just as often outside of accounts payable as they are by individuals working in accounts payable.

The issue is complicated by the fact that often wire payments are made for not-purchase order items. So, instructing organizations to use the proverbial three-way match and make sure POs and receivers are extinguished (one of the best ways to prevent duplicate payments of PO related invoices) is worthless. Since these payments are often for large dollar amounts, a duplicate payment is this arena can be costly indeed.

Very occasionally, a wire transfer will be made to cover a rush payment for an invoice that was not paid on time. When this is done, it is critical that the three-way match be completed and the purchase order and receiving document extinguished.

Here are a few controls you can add to your process to ensure wire transfers are paid only once:

1) Make sure there is adequate backup for each wire transfer, even though no three-way match is being completed. This way should someone suspect a duplicate there will be sufficient information to make that determination.

2) If possible, limit the payment type for particular vendors to one type (wire, ACH, check or p-card). If attempts are made to use another payment type, have the system alert the processor.

3) Periodically review the accounts of vendors typically paid by wire. This might include loan payments, interest payments, and leases.

4) Alert processors to vendors who are usually paid by wire so they can thoroughly research any invoice that comes in for payment using another payment vehicle.

5) Periodically run your list of wires against lists of other payments made looking for duplicates. Research any potential duplicates.

You should note that many duplicate payment auditors will automatically perform the last step as part of their recovery efforts.

Payments Made outside Accounts Payable

While wires in many companies have always been made outside accounts payable, traditionally they were the only payments not made by the accounts payable staff. Since the items covered by wires were usually pretty easy to identify, the chances of a duplicate payment slipping through were not high, assuming the organization took a few basic steps to protect itself.

The advent of ACH is changing that situation. They are cheaper than both wire transfers and paper checks and appear to be the wave of the future for corporations making payments. Approximately, 20% of all organizations have ACH payments initiated outside of accounts payable. Since the items being paid by ACH are the same as the items being paid by the accounts payable staff, problems can arise under a few circumstances. If the outside staff does not use the same strong rigid controls used by accounts payable, duplicate payments will arise. Specifically this means the staff outside accounts payable must:

1) Use the same rigid coding standards used in accounts payable;

2) Perform the three-way match; and

3) Extinguish purchase orders and receivers once the payment has been made.

If they do not follow the same standards, and an invoice appears in accounts payable, it will be paid, for the staff will have no way of knowing it had already been addressed. Thus it is imperative that those organizations making payments outside accounts payable sufficiently train the staff making those payments so duplicates don't slip through.

Recurring and Repetitive Payments

There are a whole variety of items that require the same payment to be made every month. This might include things like rent, equipment leases, loan payments etc. Depending on your industry, there might be other items as well. Rather than create a new voucher each month for the same exact payment, some organizations set these items up to be automatically paid on a recurring basis.

If care is not taken and an end date included in the arrangement, the organization could find itself paying for something it no longer was obliged to pay for. Hence it is critical that when recurring payments are set up, an end date be included rather than have them go on without a light at the end of the tunnel.

The second problem that can occur is when the item is paid off early. In the case of a loan this might be an early payment or a renegotiation to get a lower rate. In the case of a lease, occasionally the lessor will entice the lessee into a new lease for better/newer equipment or whatever. Both of these situations are fine as long as the initial payment is stopped when the new payment stream begins. More than occasionally this does not happen and the original payment continues as well as the new payment.

You can run into the same problem with repetitive payments for services, phones etc. If someone does not stay on top of these accounts the organization can find itself paying for services never used. For example, if the phone company isn't notified when a phone line is no longer needed, it will continue to bill for it. For most organizations this isn't a problem as it uses all its phone lines. But those who have a significant downsizing initiative may find themselves paying for services not being used. The same can be said for subscriptions, online services, and specialized database access for employees who have left (voluntarily or not).

Strong internal controls protect any organization. It is important to make sure yours cover not only the functions used on a regular basis but also those only used occasionally.

When Internal Controls Breakdown: The AP Practice

Even organizations that believe they have tight internal controls, more than occasionally have a breakdown in controls. That's because there are a few areas that are sometimes overlooked when it comes to implementing appropriate segregation of duties and strong internal controls. Let's take a look at five places that happens in the accounts payable process.

Breakdown #1: Master Vendor File Access

The master vendor file if handled properly can serve as a strong fortress in protecting your organization against many types of fraud and duplicate payments. However for this to work, access to it for purposes of updating existing information and adding new vendors must be severely limited.

Unfortunately, in more than a few companies anyone processing an invoice can enter a vendor into the master vendor file. They can also change data on existing vendors. Even if no one tries to play games, unlimited access inevitably means vendors in the file more than once, increased chances of duplicate and/or erroneous payments and the possibility of fraud.

While it is certainly easier to simply let processors enter new vendors as they see fit, it is not a good practice.

Breakdown #2: Not Insisting on Rigid Coding Standards

One of the most common ways an organization pays twice is when its processors all don't process invoices in the same manner. This means entering data the exact same way. In order to ensure this happens in your organization, the development of a rigid coding standard for data entry both when processing invoices and when entering data in the master vendor file is critical. It is the first line of defense.

When the coding standard is developed, it should address every possible situation that might occur in the data. This includes dealing with punctuation, abbreviations, spaces, dashes, middle initials, DBAs, invoice numbers etc.

Once the standards are developed and shared with processors, there should be a periodic check to make sure no one has developed alternate entry standards for their own personal use.

Breakdown #3: Allowing Rush (ASAP) Checks

Every business has emergencies where they must issue a

payment immediately. The key is to keep this number to an absolute minimum and employ the same strong controls and processes to the rush item as would be used on an item that goes through the normal invoice processing function. Most importantly this means entering the invoice number for the invoice and extinguishing the associated purchase order and receiving document.

Regrettably many of the rush payment requests are sadly lacking in documentation and backup making it impossible to follow standard invoice handling procedures. If this is the case, documentation should be collected after-the-fact, when it becomes available and the appropriate actions taken.

When the purchase order and receiving document remain open the likelihood of a duplicate payment (rarely returned by the vendor) skyrockets. For, without the closing of documents the (PO and or receiver), when a second invoice shows up, it appears as though the goods were not paid for and a second payment could slip through.

Breakdown #4: Returning Checks to Requisitioners

Returning checks to requisitioners is a nightmare for accounts payable as well as a sign of poor internal controls. In order to return the check, the payment must be separated out of the normal check production cycle. The entire process is inefficient adding time to a process that does not have to be. What's more, a large percentage of checks that are returned to the requisitioner are also Rush checks. So there are two potential places for internal controls to breakdown on these payments.

But the real breakdown in internal controls comes from giving the check to an employee instead of mailing it. Many cases of employee fraud involve an employee insisting on getting the payment returned to them for delivery and then keeping the check and cashing it for personal use.

One of the easiest ways to eliminate a good part of this problem is to insist that all Rush payments be made by electronic (ACH) payment not check. Then there is no check to return. A strong policy of not returning checks works wonders if backed by management. And, finally, if all else fails and there are still requests for checks to be returned, consider developing a form requiring an explanation of why the return is needed. This form should also require an additional signature from a high level executive like the CFO. Ideally, the signature required should be of an individual who supports the "No Return" policy. Just implementing a policy that will require someone to have to go and explain to the CFO does wonders in reducing the number of such requests.

Breakdown #5: Having a Petty Cash Box

Anyone who has ever run a petty cash box probably has at least one hair-raising tale to tell about shenanigans that went on with the box. Inevitably the boxes get out of balance and rarely does that misbalance result in there being more money in the box than there should be. But that's just the beginning of the nightmares associated with petty cash boxes. They are time intensive to operate, the documentation for the reimbursements from the box are often flimsy and verifying the item was reimbursed elsewhere is difficult, if not impossible.

Given the wide use of credit cards and corporate cards, there is really no reason why almost all companies who still have petty cash boxes don't eliminate them. Yet, about one-quarter of all organizations still have them. We've already alluded to the double reimbursement issue, which can be intentional or unintentional. What's more, employees will sometimes put items through the petty cash box for reimbursement that they could not get through on their travel and expense reimbursement reports because of the scrutiny of those reports. If the item can't pass muster on T&E there is absolutely no reason for it to be reimbursed through petty cash.

The simple solution to the petty cash box internal control breakdown is to eliminate it. Small expenditures can be put through the travel and expense reimbursement process.

If the organization insists on keeping a petty cash box, the amount of cash should be small, the people reimbursed through it should be limited to those who don't ever submit an expense reimbursement request and the amounts limited to a very small amount, say $10 or $25. Lastly, having a petty cash box puts the office where it is located at a slightly elevated risk for theft, if it is widely known the company has cash on its premises.

Concluding Thoughts

Strong internal controls are critical to a well-run accounts payable function. In this and other articles in this series, we've taken a look at some of the more common ways these controls break down. But these are not the only ways. Hopefully, you'll keep your eyes peeled and constantly evaluate new and existing processes to make sure your organization has the strongest controls possible.

Five Reasons Why Internal Controls Sometimes Fail and What You Can Do to Make Sure This Doesn't Happen in Your AP Department

Most accounting and finance professionals are well aware that strong internal controls are the first step towards safeguarding the organization's assets. When it comes to accounts payable, these controls guard against duplicate payments, erroneous payments and fraudulent payments. More than occasionally controls fail, not because someone is deceitful but rather due to a lack of understanding of the principles or how they should be implemented. Let's take a look at five common reasons internal controls fail.

Reason #1: Lack of appropriate review. This happens frequently with approvers signing expense reimbursement reports. Unfortunately, it also sometimes happens with purchasers approving invoices for payment.

Solution: Make managers responsible for what they

approve - really. A few organizations have gone so far as to make it a firing offense if a manager approves an obviously fraudulent expense reimbursement. Most are not willing to go that far. Some are making it a matter for consideration when calculating the annual salary increase.

Reason #2: Incomplete segregation of duties. When it comes to processing invoices for payment, it is critical that no one person can perform more than one leg of the operation. For example, someone shouldn't have the ability to enter invoices and sign checks. Too often we see companies set up the segregation of duties correctly and then make one or two "exceptions," usually for a trusted employee such as the controller or accounts payable manager. Smaller accounts payable departments are sometimes challenged when it comes to setting up processes so duties are appropriately segregated.

Solution: The first step is to realize that there can be no exceptions when it comes to separating duties. Remember internal fraud is most likely to be committed by a long term trusted employee. Regardless of the operational efficiencies that can be achieved by allowing these exceptions, the more important issue of fraud protection should override. So, allow no exceptions. Smaller organizations sometimes have to look outside accounts payable to help. Some common examples of segregating duties by taking advantage of help from other departments include putting the master vendor file elsewhere in accounting and having Treasury responsible for getting signatures put on checks (if they are not signed as part of the check printing cycle).

Reason #3: Incomplete knowledge regarding policies and procedures. Too often we don't realize the knowledge we have regarding how the accounts payable department operates has been accumulated over a long period of time. When newcomers are hired, they are typically given a day or two of training before being hurled into the mix to sink or swim. Most do a fairly good job but occasionally do miss a fine point or a procedure that only comes up once in a blue moon.

Solution: Probably the best approach any organization can take when it comes to ensuring complete knowledge about policies and procedures is to have a detailed, up-to-date policy and procedures manual. Give this to every processor as a reference guide and they can check it when those odd transactions show up. Encourage even your seasoned staff to refer to the guide when they are not 100% certain how something should be handled. Refresher training is another step you can also take to ensure you don't run into this problem.

Reason #4: Sharing passwords. It is quite tempting when an employee is heading out for vacation to ask that employee to share his/her password with another employee who will take over the vacationing employee's responsibility. Resist the temptation. This is a slippery slope and whether sharing a password for a vacation or on a regular basis, it is a bad idea. It completely obliterates the audit trail making it impossible to tell who did what.

Solution: The answer is obvious. When someone needs to take over the responsibilities of another employee, set them up with their own password. When the vacation is over and if you don't need/want that employee to have access, cancel the access. This may be an extra step but it protects your internal controls.

Reason #5: Overrides. Management overrides of transactions are an easy way to fix mistake. Unfortunately, they are also an easy way for an unscrupulous employee to adjust the records to cover up a fraud.

Solution: If at all possible, do not use management overrides to fix a problem. Go through the more laborious route of doing the correct accounting to take care of the issue, even if it means owning up to some really stupid mistakes. If your organization does not want to go that route and insists on allowing overrides, then at a minimum have a form explaining the reason for the override and have it signed by at least one executive other than the person putting through the override.

Internal controls are an important component of any organization's fraud prevention program. They also go a long way to helping ensure accurate records and financial statements. Don't let the senseless issues discussed above get in the way of your controls. Implement the solutions suggested to strengthen your controls rather than weaken them.

Chapter 7: Purchase Orders and Their Role in Internal Controls

As the title implies, purchase orders (PO) are forms, usually filled out in purchasing, that detail the parameters of a purchase transaction. They are usually sent to the supplier and in an ideal situation, a copy is also sent to accounts payable. In today's electronic environment, these forms can be transmitted electronically and/or filled in on an online database. In such cases accounts payable can and should have access. They play a critical role in maintaining strong internal controls. In this section we investigate:

- Good PO practices that insure strong controls
- Practices to control maverick spend

Purchase Orders and Appropriate Internal Controls

At the head of all accounts payable operations is the invoice processing function. In fact, given the diversity of the functions handled in accounts payable departments, some experts maintain that the only one constant across all thresholds is invoice processing responsibility.

Roughly speaking, invoices can be broken down into two categories:

1. Those requiring a Purchase Order and
2. Those without a purchase order

The purchase order is the first line of defense (as well as the first place where controls can start to go astray) in the invoice processing function.

As indicated above, the PO can either be the first line of defense or the first place where internal controls start to break down. Here are a few of the issues:

- How accurate is the information on the form?
- Is the form completely filled out?
- Are special deals documented on the PO?
- Is the PO filled out before the transaction is consummated or after the fact?
- When is the PO sent to accounts payable?

An invoice that is accurate, complete, and timely guards against an improper payment. An improper payment might be an incorrect amount or a payment to the wrong party or even worse a payment to a supplier who never delivered goods or services. Finally, there is the issue of payments for shoddy goods never ordered but delivered – a petty fraud that is ongoing (usually of copier toner, paper, or yellow pages ads).

The PO is one of the three key documents used to verify an invoice for payment. As those who work in accounts payable are well aware, the proverbial three-way match is used in most organizations. It matches the PO against the receiving documents and the invoice submitted for payment. When all three match, the invoice is processed and a payment scheduled. If there is no match, discrepancies must then be resolved.

Purchase Order Problems

Most PO problems signify a breakdown in internal controls. Accounts payable professionals who have problems getting some of these issues addressed can now use the threat of noncompliance with the Sarbanes-Oxley Act to harness management support for their initiatives. Specifically, and at a minimum, POs:

- Should be completely filled out (a big problem in some organizations)
- Sent to accounts payable (or AP should have online access)
- Not be done after the fact

If the PO does not have all the information included it is difficult if not impossible to complete the three-way match. Companies that require this matching (and that is most of them) will sometimes end up without an invoice. When alerted to this fact, the purchasing professional will sometimes create one. This is really adding work, without adding value. However, it often is necessary within the confines of the operating policy of the organization – and is a complete breakdown in internal controls. It is also a prime example of how special terms can get lost – because they are never reported to accounts payable and the vendor, either intentionally or by mistake, has created the invoice using the standard terms rather than the special terms negotiated. Thus, the hard work the purchasing professional put in getting the improved terms was for naught.

Purchase Orders for Everything

Some organizations require a PO for every payment that is made. Others require them for every material purchase made. This approach can be use to subtlety pressure employees to use payment mechanisms (e.g., p-cards and reimbursements through T&E reports) that do not require a PO.

Non Purchase Order Invoices

Purchase orders are a great internal control. However, not every purchase lends itself to the purchase order methodology. When an invoice shows up that has no PO related to it, the internal controls are weakened. However, non-PO invoices are a fact of life for many organizations. Typically they are marked, "Okay to Pay", and signed by an employee authorized to approve purchases. Sometimes these invoices are attached to a check request form and sometimes they are not.

As you can imagine, the controls on such purchases are weaker than the controls associated with a PO. Additional problems, especially with low-dollar non-PO invoices include:

- No real verification of the product received
- No verification of whether the produce was ordered, meets standards, and so forth
- No real verification as to whether this is a duplicate invoice

Purchase Orders for Everything

Some organizations require a PO for every payment that is made. Others require them for every material purchase made. This approach can be used to subtlety pressure employees to use payment mechanisms (e.g., purchasing cards [p-cards] and reimbursements through travel and entertainment [T&E] reports) that do not require a PO.

Controlling Maverick Spend

Just about every company has them. They are the folks who sometimes intentionally and sometimes not, throw a monkey wrench into the corporate spend policy by not following the guidelines. Occasionally, there is fraud involved but more often than not, that is not the case. What's more, sometimes it is senior level executives causing the problem. That can be especially tricky to handle.

How Purchase Order Analytics Can Help

The stronger the controls an organization has in place around its spend and purchase orders, the less likely this type of behavior is to occur. This type of spending typically results from one of the following three:

1. Purchases made from a supplier other than a preferred supplier, even if at a lower cost.

2. Purchases made without going through procurement, even though they should have.

3. Purchases made under questionable circumstances, either from a related source or at a higher price. It is this last category that is most likely to involve a fraudulent transaction.

Occasionally, folks from the first category who have made purchases at a lower cost are left scratching their heads wondering what they did wrong. What they fail to realize is that while the individual purchase may have been at an attractive price, it could result in a higher price for other purchases made under the preferred contract, if promised levels are not made.

So, what can you do to control this behavior?

- **Step1**. Set up clear policies defining procurement practices, especially as they relate to purchase orders.
- **Step2**. Identify your inappropriate spend and the purchasers who are responsible for it. This is where your purchase order data analytics will come in handy.
- **Step3**. Immediately, notify the appropriate managers so that the maverick behavior can be stopped.

Stopping maverick spend as soon as the cycle starts is critical. It usually costs the organization and these are funds that come right off the bottom line. The economic damage that can be done can be severe and the money rarely recovered. Therefore it is important that the data analytics be run on a very regular basis, either weekly or monthly. If you only look at your data annually, say at budget time, maverick behavior may go on for a long time doing real damage to your preferred contracts or worse. Weekly or monthly is better.

Maverick Spend by An Unlikely Source

One of the dirty little secrets in the corporate world is the identity of some of the worst non-compliers when it comes to the corporate procurement policy. Senior executives often feel their needs are "special" and that procurement really doesn't understand their "unique" requirements. For this reason they more than occasionally feel that they should be exempt from the policy and if not formally excluded then it should be understood that they won't comply. This can be especially contentious when there's corporate travel or entertainment involved. This is not to imply that fraud is involved. That's not what we're talking about.

Needless to say, this creates all sorts of problems for accounts payable when the invoices or expense reimbursement requests for their out-of-policy spend arrives. In some organizations it would be political suicide to question these invoices and so the accounts payable staff simply bites the bullet and pays them. But, really that is not the right way, it sets a bad example. Inevitably a few other employees feel they should be treated the same way and then more problems ensue.

Although it may not seem possible, this problem can be nipped in the bud before it has a chance to emerge. When the policies are first being written, or updated, get input from the senior executives so they do not feel excluded. Rather than have someone in procurement "lay down the law" which ends up with non-compliance, take a more democratic approach. This may mean recruiting the CFO, explaining the problem and why certain policies are recommended and letting that individual explain it to the other senior executives. Finally, if the CEO puts his/her stamp of approval on the policy, it's amazing how quickly everyone else will fall into line and comply. This is one of those issues that will be greatly influenced by the corporate culture of the organization.

Finally, as we alluded to above, this issue gets particularly touchy when travel and entertainment expenditures are involved. Some companies address this issue by having two travel policies. Some hospitals often have a separate policy for doctors and some companies have a separate policy for C-level executives. It is a way to allow the different treatment without opening the floodgates.

Chapter 8: Invoice Processing: The Core of the Accounts Payable Function

As the processing of invoices is the core function for accounts payable, it is time to turn our attention to that part of the process. Strong internal controls can really make a difference, while making the function as efficient as possible. In this section we examine:

- Basic invoice handling practices that ensure tight controls
- Several special invoice situations

Practices that Ensure Tight Controls

Invoice processing is the basis for the accounts payable function. Let's take a look at the best ways to approach the function.

Documentation

Start with good documentation. It may seem obvious, but it is a step that is often omitted in the process. An updated policies and procedures manual is critical for any accounts payable function that operates with an intent to have strong internal controls. Typically, these are held in each department. The PO issue straddles at least two department lines, which is one of the reasons why there is sometimes trouble.

Thus it is suggested that accounts payable and purchasing work together on the project of documenting PO requirements and the communication between the two departments over what's on the PO and how that information is disseminated to accounts payable. What formerly may have been a territorial issue can no longer be that. Information must be shared and petty interdepartmental issues must be put aside. A comprehensive set of procedural instructions will go a long way in:

- Ensuring accurate information is shared on a timely basis
- Ensuring that only payments that are supposed to be made are made
- Ensuring that each department knows what they are required to do.

Oh, yes, and good documentation is a giant step in the right direction to ensuring everyone in your department handles the same tasks in the same manner – one of the principles of strong internal controls.

Invoice Handling: Clear Instructions

While the accounts payable department has a fairly good idea of who originates POs and who to contact to strengthen weak controls, the matter is much more difficult when it comes to invoices. For starters, virtually everyone is initiated by a party outside the company's direct control. While the accounts payable department can try and lay down rules for these parties, it has little control. However, it does have strong influence in that by providing clear and accurate instructions to vendors it can hasten payments to those who conform to its guidelines.

Thus, the first step to getting invoices sent in correctly is to provide vendors with clear instructions on where invoices should be sent. This is a bigger issue than it might appear at first glance. For starters, the company needs to have a policy regarding where invoices should be sent. This breaks down into two possibilities:

1. Directly to accounts payable
2. To the individual who authorized the purchase

These are virtually the only two choices and there appears to be no right way. Companies vary on what they require. Some want everything sent to accounts payable where it may be scanned before being sent out for approval. Others require that the invoice only be sent to accounts payable only after it has been approved for payment. Which way is better? There is no clear answer as both methodologies have problems associated with them.

However, even though most experts recommend that invoices be directed to someone's attention, many come in addressed to no one and float through the company eventually ending up in accounts payable. No wonder vendors don't get paid on time! Even when the mailroom is told to forward anything that looks like an invoice to accounts payable, invoices float.

A decision regarding where invoices should be sent needs to be made within each company. Once that decision has been made this information needs to be communicated to all vendors. It should be included in the welcome package that is sent to new vendors. It can also be communicated through regular communication that purchasing has with suppliers. However, on the vendor's side, this information needs to be transferred from the sales staff to the professionals responsible for billing. If there appears to be a breakdown in communication on this issue at the supplier (and some sales people have little interest in the billing side of things), accounts payable can take the lead and communicate this to the person responsible for billing.

There is also an issue when invoices arrive in accounts payable with no indication as to who ordered the items covered by the invoice. Some companies, usually the lead players in an industry, require that either the name of the person ordering the goods or the PO number be included on the invoice. Without these vital pieces of information, accounts payable may be clueless as to where to go to get the invoice approved for payment, a very necessary part of the payment process.

Invoice Approval Process: Delegations

Typically, in a well-run company, the Board of Directors delegates the authority for various functions through resolutions. This authority can then be sub-delegated. Thus, the Board might delegate purchasing authority at various dollar levels to several high level executives, typically by title (not name). These executives then sub-delegate to their appropriate staff.

All this information should be written down and updated whenever there is a change. This information should be given to the accounts payable department. It should also contain signature specimens similar to those obtained for signature cards for the banks. This is sensitive information and should be kept in a secure location, not lying around where anyone passing by might see it. Similarly, whenever the information is updated, old copies should be destroyed.

It is important to remember that there is a difference between the person who submits something for payment and the person who approves that payment. The number of people who can submit for payment will be much higher than those who can approve. It is an internal control feature to have at least two sets of eyes view every purchase. No one should approve payments for items they have purchased.

Clearly, the number of people who can authorize a payment will be limited, even at large companies. This delegation is also limited by dollar levels. Thus, a $100 purchase may be approved by a supervisor, while a $100,000 purchase might require the authorization of a vice president.

Getting the Approval

If there is one area that causes accounts payable more headaches it is the invoice approval process. Some of the most egregious examples of how accounts payable and purchasing don't get along revolve around the invoice approval process. Here's how the scenario plays out when things are not going well. Accounts payable sends an invoice to purchasing for approval. The purchasing professional has many things to do and low on his list of priorities is checking that invoice and approving it for payment. Until it is approved and returned accounts payable can't do anything. So, it sits for weeks in purchasing getting buried deeper each day as more paper is dumped into the in-box.

Then the vendor calls looking for its payment. The purchasing guy, who wants to be the good guy and is unlikely to admit that he's been sitting on the invoice, tells the vendor to call accounts payable, that he sent it back to them weeks ago. It's a quick way to get rid of an angry vendor. He then quickly finds the invoice, signs off on it (without checking it!), puts it in an inter-office envelope marked accounts payable and forgets about the whole mess. Now, when the vendors call accounts payable, they are under the impression that their invoices have been there for weeks. So these conversations tend to be a tad on the touchy side.

In the ideal scenario, accounts payable sends the invoice to purchasing for approval (or does not receive it until it has been approved), purchasing approves it and returns it to accounts payable within 24 hours for processing for payment.

When an invoice is not paid by the end of the billing cycle (typically once a month), a follow up invoice is sent. While this may be marked COPY or DUPLICATE INVOICE, they are not always so marked. Many of these second invoices get paid, often before the original invoice winds its way back to accounts payable. And, what do you think happens when that original turns up in accounts payable, approved for payment? If you answered that it sometimes gets paid, you are correct. Getting that duplicate payment returned can be a tedious and expensive proposition.

Clearly, paying an invoice twice indicates a breakdown in internal controls. To address this issue, most companies run some sort of duplicate payment checking program to try and identify these payments before the money goes out the door. The programs have varying degrees of success, often depending on the level of controls in other parts of the accounts payable process.

The procedures for getting invoices approved, including the recommended timeframes for each step, should be documented as part of the policy and procedures manual. They should also be flow charted as part of that exercise.

Electronic processes have addressed many of these problems. See the Electronic Invoicing section for a discussion on this issue.

The Three-Way Match

As mentioned above, the three-way match is a strong control feature used at most corporations. If the PO, receiving document and approved invoice match, the item is scheduled for payment. However, frequently the three do not match and then the fun begins. It is also where the best-intentioned internal controls can start to fall apart. Discrepancies can and should be investigated by the party in the best position to resolve them. That is rarely accounts payable, yet this is often where the responsibility for dispute resolution lies.

Strong dispute resolution mechanisms and policies should be developed. This can be helped along greatly if invoice automation is used. Some of the electronic invoicing modules currently on the market incorporate an online dispute resolution mechanism which is extremely helpful.

Discrepancies in the three-way match process can be tracked by vendor and approver to identify potential weak links in the PO and approval process. Once it becomes clear that there is an issue with a particular vendor or purchaser, steps can be taken to eliminate the root cause of the problem. Sometimes, all that is needed is a little education.

Special Invoice Situations

It would be wonderful if all invoices could be handled in exactly

Internal Controls in Accounts Payable

the same manner. However, there are a few situations that may require special handling. Let's take a look at two of them.

Handling Small-Dollar Invoices

Small dollar invoices are the bane of many accounts payable departments. They take a considerable amount of time and energy to process, taking precious time from larger transactions that deserve more scrutiny. Thus, many companies encourage the use of p-cards for small dollar transactions. Others have developed mechanisms to review these invoices in a manner that utilizes fewer precious resources. One example is negative assurance. Approvers are notified of an invoice but not required to take any action unless they did not order the goods in question, hence the negative connotation in the nomenclature.

While these approaches are probably good from a work flow standpoint, they do open the door for potential small dollar fraud, if care is not taken. Thus, while it is makes sense from an operational standpoint to implement these processes, extreme care needs to be taken to ensure that the appropriate controls are put in at the same time. Otherwise, the fraudsters will quickly hone in on your weak links.

Dealing with Invoices without Invoice Numbers

Many non PO invoices, as well as some invoices associated with POs, have no invoice number. While to the uninitiated this may seem like a minor issue, it can create huge control issues. In fact, invoices without invoice numbers is one of the leading causes of duplicate payments. The reason for this is that in many organizations the controlling feature on determining if a payment has been made is the invoice number.

Without that feature, the controls go out the window – unless a strict numbering standard has been established to issue invoice numbers to these invoices. An even better approach is to require a purchase order number on all invoices. By returning invoices to the vendor that are received without a purchase order number or name of a requisitioner with a polite letter explaining you need this information on all invoices in order to get them paid quickly, you will address this issue. While there may have been a time that this might have been seen as an unusual request, it is no longer the case. There is no reason for any company to send invoices without invoice numbers.

Chapter 9: Invoice-Related Control Issues

The way invoices are handled in AP has changed dramatically in the last five to ten years and continues to change as organizations in growing numbers look to automation to improve productivity. The key for these firms is to make sure that the changes do not weaken controls. The good news is that often the new changes actually strengthen controls. Let's examine:

- Some practices that ensure tight controls around invoice processing
- Contract compliance
- Electronic invoicing
- The fiscal period closes

Recommended Invoice Processing Practices to Ensure Tight Controls

To ensure the fewest control issues in your invoice handling practices, use the following practices:

- Pre-number and account for all purchase orders

- Match invoices, receiving and purchase order information and follow up on missing or inconsistent information

- Record invoices accurately on a timely basis for all accepted purchases that have been authorized

- Restrict ability to modify data

- Reconcile vendor statements

- Implement standards to guard against inaccurate input of

data

• Follow up on unmatched open purchase orders, receiving reports, and invoices and resolve missing, duplicate, or unmatched items, by individuals independent of purchasing and receiving functions

• Have a focus for action/control activities

• Uncover and take action quickly on invalid accounts payable fraudulently created for unauthorized or nonexistent purchase.

Contract Compliance

As companies everywhere look for ways to cut costs and improve efficiency, one area that continues to offer potential for some real bottom line enhancements is the area of contract compliance. This is especially true of organizations that have large complicated contracts involving many different items. The obvious example that springs to mind is a hospital that orders many different types of suppliers and different drugs. The opportunities for volume discounts are numerous.

Often these contracts go on for pages and rarely are invoices checked against contracts to make sure that all the terms of the contract are taken advantage of. It will come as no surprise to most reading this to learn that the more complicated the contract, the less likely it is that a company will adhere to it even most of the time. In fact, there are organizations whose business offering is simply going through contracts and payments, finding discrepancies and then recovering those overpayments.

Again, the goal in this arena is to identify those potential overpayment situations before the funds are disbursed. A few companies have set up contract compliance groups, most often as part of purchasing, but occasionally under the accounts payable umbrella. This group is charged with making sure that the invoices paid comply with the signed contract. On the face of it, this may seem like a fairly straightforward process. Going back to the hospital example, it is easy to see how prices, especially in heavily negotiated supplies, could be misquoted. Equally important are the terms and any potential penalties. And, as mentioned elsewhere in this chapter, special deals that are arranged outside the master contract.

Contract compliance reviews go hand in hand with strong internal controls and good documentation. For most companies, this is a relatively untapped arena that offers one of the last few footholds for professionals to find cost savings for their firms. To be done correctly, this needs to be one or more individuals' prime responsibility – not something to be handled off the side of their desks in the slow time (whenever that may be in accounts payable!).

Master Vendor File Basics Related to Invoices

The master vendor file is the repository of all significant information about the company's suppliers. It is the reference point for accounts payable when it comes to paying invoices – and if handled incorrectly it can (and does) lead to massive problems. Fraud and duplicate payments are just the tip of the iceberg. While a company may have been willing to live with those risks in the past, they risk getting a negative assessment in their Sarbanes-Oxley audit if they continue to employee the poor practices with regard to their master vendor files.

At a minimum, to have any chance of not being dinged when their master vendor file practices are reviewed, a company should:

- Limit access to the master vendor file
- Periodically disable inactive vendors in the file (but do not delete the entries as the payment history associated with that vendor needs to be retained)
- Establish a naming convention to be used when setting up vendors initially
- Require that certain information (like W-9s) be obtained before the vendor can be set up and/or paid

- Have a regular review (yes, I know it is boring work) of all changes made to the file

The reason for the last requirement is that more than one thieving employee has been known to go into the master vendor file to change the mailing address to divert a legitimate payment from the vendor to an unintended party, usually themselves. Then, once the check has been mailed, they go back into the file and change the address back to the correct mailing address. Without the review of the changes, the fraud could go on undetected for years, with different vendors being targeted each time.

Electronic Invoicing

Many of the problems facing the accounts payable function can be addressed through the use of electronic invoicing. For starters, the blame game that typically surrounds who got the invoice when, dissipates in the face of electronic workflow systems which not only leaves an audit trail for everyone to see but also often includes an automatic escalation to the approver's boss should he or she be on vacation – or simply be neglectful of their responsibilities related to checking and approving invoices for payment.

Similarly, there can be no dispute over who received an invoice and the timing of that receipt. Likewise, the electronic feature lets accounts payable forward the invoice for approval without having to rely on the often dubious interoffice mail facilities. This also relieves them of the onerous task of making copies before the invoice is forwarded and then having to dig through that file to determine what's been returned, where the invoice is in the approval chain, how long it's been out there, what needs to be followed up on, and so on. All these tasks add no value and even worse, zap departmental productivity.

As you have probably figured out the process described above does not demonstrate anything remotely resembling strong internal controls and worse is an invitation to fraud and duplicate payments. The process is not conducive to timely reporting and getting the books closed at month end and the end of the fiscal year can be a real challenge as more accruals than should be necessary have to be prepared. The accountants reading this will point out that it is much better to record an invoice on the books than to try and accrue for it.

Evaluation

If it seems like we don't think electronic invoicing is a good thing, we gave you the wrong impression. We think the advantages far outweigh some of the smaller problems they may create. The huge advantage in the electronic invoicing world is the models that come with an online dispute resolution mechanism. This allows for discrepancies to be adjudicated in a timely manner and for payment to be made in an equitable time frame.

And, while I recognize that a small number of companies use disputes to "legitimatize" their poor payment practices, from a Sarbanex-Oxley and an internal controls standpoint, it is not a good practice. By leaving invoices unpaid for long periods of time the odds of fraud and duplicate payment increase. Additional accruals may need to be done which do not enhance the timely reporting and disclosure requirements.

e-Mailed Invoices

Not all invoices delivered electronically come through an electronic invoicing model. Just about every organization receives at least a few invoices via e-mail. Typically these are an attached pdf file of the invoice. Many third-party systems can take these pdfs and read them into their own process.

Most organizations not using a third party model still take invoices via e-mail. For them, there is a new control issue. Some vendors, in their zeal to make sure their invoices arrive, are both e-mailing (or faxing) their invoices, as well as mailing them through the postal service. Thus it is more imperative than ever that all organizations have good controls in place to identify those second invoices.

For without good controls, some of those second invoices will get paid. As discussed earlier, most vendors do not return duplicate payments unless prompted by a reminder either from the customer or its third party audit firm.

Fiscal Period Closes: The Month-End Close

In the ideal environment, there would be no accruals needed. Of course, in the real world that is unlikely to happen, no matter how good a company's processes are. The requirements for the issuance of financial statements are tight and cannot be met if individual reporting units, such as accounts payable, do not close their books on a timely basis.

In addition to the timeliness issue is the question of internal controls in the invoicing process. If the process of closing the books drags out, it can be a reflection of the adequacy of the internal controls – and not a positive one.

Fiscal Period Closes: Year-End Close

Everything that applies to the month end close is applicable to the year-end close in spades. Timely reporting and strong internal controls come into play. The year-end close may also have an ugly sub-certification requirement associated with it. Thus, it is important the professional who signs that document ensure that not only is the work done, but the internal controls are adequate.

Making the Close Run a Little Smoother

December and January do not have to be any more hectic than the rest of the year. Of course, for that to happen you have to take the appropriate steps to get ready before the year-end train comes hurling down the tracks once again wreaking havoc in its wake. Here are a few steps you can take to ensure a smoother year end.

1. Hire an intern to work over the holidays. If you have a few dollars left in your budget, hire a college student to

help out over the holidays and perhaps in January while the student is on winter break. The student will appreciate the income and you will be able to get some of the more tedious work cleared out. In fact, if you post a notice on the company bulletin board, an employee in another department may have a child or niece or nephew that fits the bill. This is also a good way to try out a prospective employee.

2.   Get travel & entertainment processing and reimbursements caught up. Few people travel towards the end of the year, especially after December 15, so this is a good time to get T&E processing up to date. You might send reminders out to all travelers telling them to get their reimbursement requests in before December 10 (or whatever date appropriate for your organization) if they wish to be reimbursed before December 20 (or the appropriate date for your organization). Your goal is to make sure that you are not dealing with rush T&E requests on the last few days of the year when you are trying to get accounts payable's books closed.

3.   Try to get all invoices into accounts payable as early in the month as possible. Then get them all entered into the system. If you have a backlog, the intern discussed in step one will help. This will help with your accrual process as well as improve the accuracy of those accruals.

4.   Don't leave year end reviews until the last minute. You know they're coming, so get them started in November— at least how the raise and promotion budget will be allocated along with all the paper work. Whether you tell your employees or not will depend on company policy.

5.   December is a terrible time for Rush checks. Send a notice saying no Rush checks will be issued and all invoices need to be delivered to AP before December 20 (or the appropriate date for your group). Do not expect to be 100% successful with this initiative but if you can

reduce the number of invoices arriving on the 30th and 31st, you will have made the close a little smoother.

6. Stop wasting time in December trying to track down the social security numbers of the independent contractors used during the year. If you do not already have a policy of requiring a W-9 from every vendor before you do business with them, institute it now. It puts an end to the December/January madness that sometimes accompanies the issuance of 1099.

7. Stop wasting time in the fall to reconcile discrepancies reported by the IRS on B-Notices, those awful notices the IRS sends to let you know the information you filed earlier in the year was not correct. Mismatches between the name and the taxpayer identification number are frequent. Reduce your mismatches to almost nothing by participating in the IRS TIN Matching program and using it throughout the year.

8. Make approving invoices for payment and returning them to accounts payable for processing a top priority. This will make AP run smoother with fewer vendor inquiries, improve vendor relations and reduce duplicate payments, making your organization more profitable.

None of the strategies recommended here is earth shattering; all are within the realm of everyone reading this. By implementing them you will improve the efficiency of the accounting department and perhaps have employees who are a little less harried.

Closing Thoughts

The invoice is where the payment process starts. It is therefore crucial that appropriate controls are incorporated at this stage. Otherwise, the door to fraud and duplicate payments is opened. Additionally, when thinking about segregation of duties as it relates to the payment process, it is imperative that the invoice handling phase be included in that equation. Otherwise, true segregation of duties may not be achieved.

Chapter 10: When Paying by Check:
The Internal Control Migraine

When most people think about accounts payable, checks immediately come to mind. It is also the area in accounts payable that may be most vulnerable to weak controls. If proper attention isn't paid, control weaknesses will permeate the process. In this section, we explore:

- The best way to handle checks with strong internal controls
- Check stock
- Check signing and mailing

Check Issuance from a Strong Control Perspective

How much problems there are around the check production process will depend upon the corporate culture of an organization. Depending on the size of the organization, segregation of duties can also be an issue when it comes to check related activities. For example, did you know that the person who handles the bank account reconciliation function should not be involved in unclaimed property reporting?

If you are scratching your head over that one, the explanation is relatively straightforward. The person who reconciles the bank accounts could indicate on the bank reconciliation reports that an item had been escheated (turned over to the state). In reality he or she simply reissued the check to a friend or themselves. This example demonstrates just how easy it can be for a dishonest individual knowledgeable about a company's inner workings to commit fraud.

Authorized Signers and Board Delegations

The authority to sign checks typically is set by the Board of Directors. This generally indicates who, by title, can sign and to what dollar limits. This authorization can typically be sub-delegated and in most cases the Board authorization will indicate whether the signer can delegate further.

The Board authorizations should also indicate whether one or two signatures are required on each check, at what levels a second signature is required, if a facsimile signature may be used, and so on.

Authorized Signers

In some companies, every executive over a certain level, say vice president, will be made an authorized signer on all bank accounts. This is viewed as a perk of the position, kind of an honorary thing. It is also a terrible practice from an internal control standpoint – although this is a battle that most accounts payable managers are loath to start.

To ensure accuracy accounts payable should keep a list of authorized signers by bank account. This list is often the same one that lists all the company's bank account numbers. Many times the signers are the same on all accounts so only one list is maintained. There are several control points that surround this issue. Before adding anyone to the list, some analysis should be given to the consideration of whether the organization gains anything by adding this individual. Will they really be available to sign in cases of emergency or is that just wistful thinking or an excuse to add an executive who thinks he or she should be on the list? Clearly this is an issue that the accounts payable manager needs to address gingerly.

Documentation: Check Signers and Accounts

First, the report with all the sensitive information should have a limited distribution. This is a need-to-know report not one that should be distributed to everyone who might have a passing interest in the data. Again, just because someone is a vice president does not mean that they need this information. If the individual is not going to be writing or signing checks, then they probably do not need to be on the distribution list for this report. While this may sound harsh, it is in the company's best interest.

The list should be kept in a concealed location not out on the desk of a clerk where anyone passing by can see it. And, in the evening it should not be left out on a desk, even in an office, where someone on the cleaning staff could see it.

As mentioned, the distribution of the report should be limited and whoever is responsible for generating it should keep a list of who received the report. It's a good control point to mark the report with a statement asking that it not be copied. All the controls fly out the window if one of the recipients takes the report and makes copies for people specifically excluded from receiving the report. Don, the vice president in R&D, does not need to know that the controller is one of the backup signers.

Whenever a new report is generated, the old reports should be returned and destroyed. While you can ask the recipients to destroy their copies, a super careful manager would get the reports back and destroy them himself.

The list needs to be updated every time there is a change. And, those changes include when an employee, who is an authorized signer leaves the firm. At that point, anyone with any responsibility for getting checks signed as well as the banks should be notified that the employee has left. This is an area that is often overlooked. This control is especially important if the employee in question was terminated or leaves disgruntled. Often notifying the bank and accounts payable is last on the list of things that anyone thinks about. It is crucial in those organizations that insist on putting every Tom, Dick, and Harry on the authorized signer list.

One last control point when it comes to check signers. If an employee who is also an authorized signer departs under unpleasant circumstances, the organization might want to consider closing all bank accounts on which that person was a signer. Yes, it's an expensive option but the losses that might occur with check fraud could far outweigh the cost, especially if blank laser stock is used. If the company is still using expensive preprinted check stock, this could be a costly and time-consuming solution.

Check Stock

Handled incorrectly, an organization's check stock can open the door to fraud. If the stock is managed in a prudent manner the risk is reduced. Readers are probably aware that even if they do everything correctly they still stand a good chance of being hit with fraudulent checks.

Laser versus Preprinted

The first matter to be decided is what kind of check stock should be used. This is probably the first control issue related to the check itself. In the business environment, paper checks come in two varieties: preprinted and laser stock.

Most everyone is familiar with preprinted checks. They come with the vital information already printed on them. They are also pre-numbered. Ideally they incorporate some security features to make fraud a little more difficult. They require a good deal of management because in the hands of the wrong individual they can be lethal. Corporations with numerous subsidiaries, each having their own bank account, can have a massive storage and control issue on their hands, if they use preprinted check stock. Still, many organizations, and virtually all individuals use preprinted check stock.

Laser checks, however, have none of the vital information pre-printed on them. Before printing, they are simply a piece of paper. While in theory, a company using a laser check printing approach could use blank typing paper, this is not recommended and few, if any, do. Rather laser checks, although printed by a regular laser printer, are printed on special safety paper, which is often numbered. This numbering is not to be confused with the check number. Rather it is a control feature on the back of the item and is used by the organization in question to control its stock. Since the vital information is printed on the check at the time the check is printed, an organization with numerous entities does not need to purchase separate check stock for each one. Similarly, when an account is closed, there is no stock to be destroyed.

Let me make one thing clear. While there are many advantages from a business standpoint to laser checks, using pre-printed check stock does not mean an organization has poor internal controls and is therefore not in compliance with Sarbanes-Oxley. What it does mean however, is that organizations that use preprinted check stock will have to exercise a far higher number of internal controls in order to be in compliance with the Act.

Security Features

Controls on the check process start with the safety or security features built into the check itself. There are over 20 different security features that an organization can incorporate into its check. It is not necessary to incorporate all of them to be considered to have decent internal controls in the check stock itself. It is generally considered a reasonable business practice to have at least three such features in your check stock. Less than that and your checks could be considered suspect if there was a check fraud.

Here's one last note about security features. Sometimes, in an effort to cut costs, organizations will order their checks from an outfit that offers an inexpensive product. A check's a check, goes the rationalization. While I don't recommend spending any more than necessary, don't cut your costs at the expense of security.

Storage

Do you keep the spare checkbooks for your organization's bank accounts in your desk drawer or in an unlocked filing cabinet in the departmental work area? If you do, you have a bit of company, so don't feel bad on that count. However, if your auditors uncover this during their audits, they will ding you on the internal control issue. Now before you dismiss this issue as something that would not happen under your watch, think about the checkbook you use to reimburse petty cash and the one used to write quick checks to employees who are terminated. Where are they kept in your organization?

Check stock should be kept under lock and key with extremely limited access. This is another example of where all the executives in the department do *not* need a key to the check storage area. The more people who have access to the location, the less secure it actually is. Some organizations limit that access to two individuals. Those individuals should not leave the key to the storage area in their desks so "someone else can get in should they be absent." This policy effectively undoes the internal control structure.

When it comes to segregation of duties, anyone who is a check signer should not also have access to the check storage area. In most organizations the responsibility for the check stock area lies with a middle manager.

Check Signing and Mailing Procedures

If you take a look at the checks signed by most organizations, the first thing you will notice is they are not actually signed by hand, they are machine signed. This is often referred to as a facsimile signer. Typically, it is the signature of a senior executive who is one of the check signers. When signature cards are given to the bank, a signature card of the facsimile also needs to be provided.

As a control feature, many organizations require a second signature on all checks over a certain dollar limit. This limit varies widely from organization to organization. There is no right answer here. Whenever a check is given to an executive for signature, the backup for that item should accompany the check. Otherwise, frankly, it is a pointless exercise. Now this is not to say that all executives check that backup.

As many reading this are well aware, often the executive signs whatever is placed in front of him (or her). And this is not to say that accounts payable professionals don't take advantage of this. If they have a rush check and they want a quick signature, they will look for the signer who signs first and asks questions later – if ever. While this is not great from a control standpoint, it is a fact of life.

Checks being passed around for hand signature should also be kept in a secure manner. It is not uncommon to see piles of checks waiting for signature lying on an executive's desk or worse, out on the secretary's desk in an open area. This should be a control issue. It is also an opportunity for anyone walking by to flitch a check.

Once the checks are signed they should be returned for processing immediately. Otherwise, another potential weak link has been introduced into the process. The point of enumerating what can go wrong is to give the professionals responsible for the process some ammunition to get the processes improved.

There are some segregation of duties issues associated with who can sign checks and who can do other tasks. So before adding someone to the approved check signer list, evaluate what that person's other responsibilities are.

Facsimile Signer: Rubber Stamps

The first facsimile signer was probably the rubber stamp. Going back maybe 20 years it was an accepted practice to have a stamp made up with the authorized signer's signature. As anyone who has ever used one of these knows, it was frequently given to the signer's secretary who then signed away – even when the executive was out of the office and never saw the items in question. Today, not only is this not considered a good practice, it is among the very worst a company can employ.

Not only is an organization using one considered to be using inadequate controls, it will forfeit all its legal protections for check fraud. Companies using these stamps are considered negligent and therefore responsible for the entire loss, if check fraud occurs. So, if your organization is using them, make it your top priority to eliminate their use as quickly as possible.

Other Facsimile Signers

Typically, the facsimile signer is a plate that is put in either the computer that prints the checks or a separate facsimile signing machine. It contains the authorized signature and is used for signing checks. It is an authorized signer. Therefore, extreme care must be given to the storage and use of that plate. Placed in the wrong hands, it makes check fraud extremely easy.

The same care that is given to check stock should be given to the facsimile signer, sometimes referred to as a plate. And from a control and segregation standpoint, the signature plate should be kept separate from the check stock. In an ideal situation where the staff is large enough, different individuals should have responsibility for the check stock and the signature plate or machine.

Leaving the signature plate in the machine unattended can be a control issue. Leaving it in the machine (be it a printer or a check signing machine) all the time is an open invitation to fraud, if the machine is not in a secure location. Remember, any blank piece of paper can be used to generate a check.

Mailing Checks

Not everyone realizes that how checks are handled after they are printed and signed could be a control point. Leaving checks lying all day in the mailroom is a really bad idea. Why? In many organizations a large number of individuals, including temps and employees from other companies, could pass through the facility. If an individual who has larceny in his or heart happens through and sees a stack of envelopes clearly containing checks waiting to be mailed, it will be a huge temptation. So, if you must use the company mailroom facilities, do not deliver the checks until right before the mail is taken to the post office.

Just because you are not taking the checks to the mailroom, does not mean you have fulfilled your internal control issues. Don't leave the checks lying around the accounts payable department either.

Now if you think we are making too big an issue of this matter and that your company's checks are mailed in discrete envelopes, ask yourself the following question. Does your firm mail checks either in window envelopes or does it print and seal the check in an envelope in one process? Either indicates that a check could be enclosed to someone looking to steal checks.

Chapter 11: Check Related Control Issues

Without a doubt, checks are an important part of the payment landscape, for virtually every organization. For no matter how much some of us would like to be completely paperless, that doesn't seem to be in the cards for some time to come. For the foreseeable future we will all have to deal with paper checks, for at least part of our payment process. In this section we look at:

- Controls around Checks
- Rush checks
- Returning checks to requisitioners

Strengthening Controls around Checks

No company can have too many controls around your check production process. This is not an area to let things slide. In this section we investigate the proper use of check request form, positive pay, the importance of timely bank reconciliations and the handling of recurring payments.

Check Request Forms

When a payment needs to be made and there is no invoice, companies typically use a form to initiate the payment. This is another area that tends to have some control issues and it can be the source of duplicate payments and fraud. While in an ideal world, there would be no need for check request forms that is not the reality of the world in which we live.

Controls should be built around the check request form process to ensure that they are not inadvertently written for an item that will later be paid with a check. That's another way that duplicate payments occur.

Check request forms are also a way that employee fraud is occasionally perpetrated. The very nature of the check request form makes it vulnerable to breakdown in controls.

The backup requirements for check requests are often laxer than they should be. However that is starting to change, thanks to Sarbanes-Oxley. When the *Accounts Payable Now & Tomorrow* newsletter polled a group of its readers, almost half indicated that they had strengthened their backup requirements for check requests because of the Act.

Use of Positive Pay

As those reading this are probably quite aware, check fraud in the United States is a huge problem. The very best protection against check fraud is a product called Positive Pay. With this product, at the time a company does a check run, it also produces a file containing the check numbers and dollar amounts for delivery to its bank. The bank then verifies each check presented for payment against this file. If it is not on the file, the check is not honored.

Some banks take the use of positive pay so seriously that they give their corporate clients a written offer. That letter asks them to use positive pay or sign that they have decided not to use it. By refusing the product, the company is giving up a lot of its protections against check fraud.

In response to crooks who understood how positive pay worked and adjusted their check frauds to get around it, some banks now offer what is known as payee name positive pay. In addition to the dollar amount and check number, the file contains the name of the payee. This is a much stronger control for those guarding against fraud.

Timely Reconciliation of Bank Statements

Before Sarbanes-Oxley, timely reconciliation of bank statements was required if a company wanted to have any chance of not being liable for fraud, should it occur. After the Act was enacted, that issue became clearer, although again timely reconciliation of bank statements is not spelled out in the Act. However, failure to do so will result in potential frauds going undetected, not being able to reverse unauthorized ACH (automated clearinghouse) debits and loss of check fraud protections.

Now many reading this may think that this is not a problem at their firms, that they have a group or person responsible for the reconciliations and they work pretty autonomously and rarely cause a fuss. Check and make sure they are no more than 30 days behind. If the backlog is any greater, you have forfeited your protections and may get dinged on the Sarbanes-Oxley audit.

There is a new concern that is causing many best-practice organizations to reconcile their bank statements even more quickly. Because of advances in electronic payment fraud, organizations are now advised to reconcile bank accounts on a daily basis. That is because banks must be notified within 24 hours of unauthorized ACH transactions in order to guarantee the return of the funds. Since the bank recs have to be done anyway, this is not seen as a great hardship but rather a reorganizing of the work. And, on the bright side, it's often easier to find a mistake when looking at one day's activity instead of 30 all at once.

Recurring Payments

When you think of recurring payments rent jumps to mind immediately. These are fixed payments made on a periodic basis, usually but not always, monthly. Loan payments and lease payments can fall under this umbrella, as well. Savvy professionals looking to streamline their payables operations often set these recurring payments up for automatic payment, either by having a check issued in the appropriate check production cycle or scheduling an ACH credit for the appropriate amount. Often these payments do not have a maturity date. Hence, in theory, they could go on forever.

And, the evergreen feature is where the first control issue arises. There can be issues even without an evergreen feature In the case of a loan, that is either paid in full or prepaid, or a lease that is terminated, the payments will continue unless the system is notified to stop. In the case of a loan or lease, the maturity is often programmed in. Thus, it is important to incorporate strong controls to ensure that payments stop when the lease or loan matures or is prepaid.

Concluding Thoughts

The payment cycle is fraught with "opportunities" for those with thieving hearts to exploit weaknesses in less than perfect systems. To limit the opportunities for fraud as well as to meet Sarbanes-Oxley requirements, internal controls need to be strong, duties need to be fully segregated, and care needs to be taken.

Rush Checks: A Control Nightmare

If asked what function they would most like to remove from their accounts payable department, over 80% of all accounts payable professionals would probably pick rush checks, sometimes referred to as ASAP or manual checks. These are checks issued outside the normal payment cycle. Typically they are drawn when the payee must be paid before the next check run. Reasonable excuses for these items include the sudden termination of an employee, expenses as closings that cannot be forecast with any certainty, and checks to vendors when the original invoice was never received. It is the last item that causes all the headaches.

Regardless of the reason for the manual check, they cause a

disruption in the workflow of the department and for that reason are costly. Because they are handled outside the check cycle, certain tasks must be performed twice to ensure that the company's records are updated correctly. If positive pay is used (and as you will read shortly, it should be) the bank must be notified or the payee will not be able to cash the check. Rush checks are one of the leading causes for duplicate payments and fraud because of the breakdown in normal internal controls associated with the check production cycle.

As alluded to above, there are legitimate reasons for issuing an ASAP check. If the original invoice was not received and hence payment not made and the vendor is a key supplier threatening to put the organization on credit hold, a strong case can be made for issuing the check. This is especially true if not issuing it will result in a deficit of a key production ingredient that will bring a manufacturing facility to a halt. Unfortunately, at least for the accounts payable department, many times when the vendor is threatening credit hold, it is not really because the original invoice was never received. Rather it was received and disappeared into that black hole known as the approval process in purchasing. Of course, purchasing is telling the vendor that accounts payable is the abyss where its invoice was lost – but that is another story for another book.

The reality is at many organizations rush checks are routinely issued to cover the hides of professionals who have fallen down on their jobs in a variety of other departments. And, often, management refuses to back accounts payable's requests to not issue rush checks. That is starting to change in a number of organizations as these management teams realize they could get dinged in their Sarbanes-Oxley audits if they routinely permit rush checks to be issued when purchasing neglects to review invoices submitted for payment in a timely manner. If this has not yet occurred to your management team, add this to your list of reasons that rush checks should be limited. It really is an internal control point.

Reducing The Number of Rush Checks

It's an old problem; but one that many of our readers still grapple with: the Rush check issue. While Rush checks make for an inefficient payment process and lead to duplicate payments, there is an even more alarming, and often over-looked component to the problem. Rush checks are often returned to the requisitioner so he or she can make the payment personally. This is an internal control concern and one method used by unscrupulous employees to perpetrate fraud. Best practices require that checks be mailed not returned to an employee for hand delivery. So what can you do to reduce the number of Rush checks you issue? Here are three simple tactics that should help.

Talk to the Requester

When approached with a rush check request, which is almost always presented as an emergency, ask a few questions. Find out when the payment is due. If the requestor has the invoice make sure the response matches the information on the invoice. Sometimes people think there is an emergency when there really isn't one. If your check run is in one or two days, ask if the payment can wait a day or two.

Before you turn down someone with a request, find out the real reason the emergency check is needed and what caused the delay. With that information you will be able to make a good business decision regarding the ASAP check.

If you determine management will ultimately overrule your decision not to issue the check, reconsider your refusal. If you want to make a point, go ahead. Otherwise be magnanimous and get all the brownie points you can out of it. Take the opportunity to discuss the reasons you dislike rush checks and why it is bad for the organization as a whole.

Insist on Mailing the Payment

Occasionally, the request for the rush check is really just an attempt to get around a no-check-return-to-requestor policy. Once the requester realizes the check will not be returned for delivery but will be mailed, they may back down on their request. Even if they don't, you will not receive future "Rush requests" for phantom reasons.

If you have trouble getting management to agree on a No-Return-to-Requisitioner policy, look to your auditors for support. Both your internal and/or external auditors should back you 100% on this issue.

Better Yet, Insist on ACH

Finally, if you have been trying to move the vendor in question to electronic payments without much success, insist the payment be made electronically. When the vendor sees how quickly it gets paid, it may opt to sign on for electronic payments all the time. This is an every-problem-presents-an-opportunity approach. It is also a way to get problematic vendors converted to electronic payments.

While we recognize that Rush checks in all likelihood will never go away completely, these tactics should provide the ammunition to get the number down significantly.

Some Additional Tactics

If you want to put a serious dent in the number of rush checks issued in your organization, try the following:

- Convince management that they really are a bad idea. Use the facts discussed in this section along with some numbers demonstrating just how expensive a rush check actually is.

- Make it *really* difficult for someone to get a rush check. This could include requiring a sign-off from the CFO along with an explanation of why this payment could not wait for the regular check cycle. If the CFO is a believer in eliminating rush checks, this step alone may do the trick.

- Identify the causes for rush checks by keeping a log of who requests them and why. After you have a few weeks or months activity, you should be able to identify trends and culprits (both at your company and on the outside) and then fix the problem.

- Identify duplicate payments made with a rush or manual check. Bring this to the attention of everyone involved and management. There's nothing like seeing a large-dollar amount associated with rush checks to put an end to the practice.

- Insist on paying electronically instead of by check. When you do get a request for a rush check, insist on ACH payment. Hopefully you will convince the recipient to be paid electronically in the future eliminating them from future rush check pools.

By relentlessly keeping after the issue and refusing to let it grow you can make some serious headway in reducing the number of those time-wasting, productivity-sucking, rush check requests.

Returning Checks to Requisitioners

Returning checks to requisitioners is a really poor practice. Yet it persists in many organizations for a variety of reasons. Not only does it make the accounts payable function inefficient and leads to duplicate payments, it frequently makes it easier for an employee to defraud the organization. Thus, many organizations have a policy of never returning checks.

It is recommended to organizations who have a few executives adamant about this issue that they enlist the support of the audit team on this issue. Internal audit as well as outside auditors should be able to explain why returning checks to requisitioners is such a poor practice.

What You Can Do to Ensure No Hanky Pankey

As our readers are aware, returning checks to requisitioners is a sign of poor internal controls. The reason for this is simple. The return of a check to a requisitioner rather than the payee makes is easier for the person getting the check to keep it rather than give it to the intended payee. Obviously, most employees won't pull this stunt but a very few will. Moreover, returning checks creates additional work for accounts payable. And, finally, these checks get lost more frequently than checks mailed to the recipient. Understanding why checks shouldn't be returned doesn't help when presented with a situation where it appears the check must be returned. Let's take a look at three of those instances and see how they can be handled effectively.

The Attachment Issue

One of the semi-legitimate reasons employees ask for a check to be returned to them is that they need to attach it to some other material. This may be a conference registration, a subscription form, or something like that. While we are loathe to recommend anything that will add to the administrative burden in accounts payable, this is one time when, alas, that is what we are going to do.

Set up a process that allows employees to send along material that must be included with the check and then make it part of the check mailing process that these items be reattached to the check prior to the mailing.

Checks at Closings

This issue occurs most frequently with real estate transactions but it is not exclusive to them. What's even more aggravating about this problem is often these checks end up being Rush items because the exact amount isn't known until the last minute. Larger amounts are often paid by wire transfer but when it comes down to filing fees the local municipalities often require a paper check.

Clearly you are going to have to issue the check and give it to your organization's representative. Create a form that is signed not only by the person requesting the check but by that person's superior. This is one way to ensure the check is required and there are more than one set of eyes viewing the request. It is likely to deter some potential frauds.

Finally, you should be able to get some sort of a receipt from the person or entity receiving the payment. This can be delivered back to accounts payable the day following the closing. It verifies that the check was delivered to the payee. Yes, this is more work again for accounts payable but it will help strengthen your internal controls.

The Rebate Check Issue

In some companies, rebates are offered to customers making purchases over a certain amount in a given time period, usually either a quarter or a year. Sometimes the sales rep likes to deliver these checks in person as a way of securing a new order. In fact, we know of one organization where the president delivers these checks in person. While the intent is quite valid there are potential problems – both in your own organization and at the customers' end. The purchasing person who receives the payment may forget to turn the check over to be deposited or worse. Ideally, these payments should be mailed.

However, sometimes you are not in a position to "fight City Hall" and find that you must hand over the checks. As with the closing issue discussed above, have a special form created that requires a second signature when an employee requests a check.

You can also try getting a receipt. In this case you'll have to create a receipt form asking sales to have it signed when the rebate is turned over. Some sales folks will be amenable to this and others will dig their heels in and refuse. Hopefully your auditors and management will back you up on this request.

Closing Thoughts

You can also try talking to employees who want their checks returned to find out the reason behind these requests. Sometimes you will be able to suggest an acceptable alternative. For example, occasionally an executive needs a check to present to a charitable organization. We've all seen the televised events with the executive presenting a huge

Mary S. Schaeffer

facsimile of a check. You can create a similar, albeit not so large, reproduction for your executives to use.

Sometimes by talking with the person you will be able to convince them that your procedures in accounts payable will accommodate whatever their reason is and they don't really need the check returned.

Of course, the best solution to this problem is to convert as many vendors to ACH for payment purposes. Amazingly, in some organizations with a history of slow payments, the requestor is concerned about getting the payment to the customer on time. They believe by getting the check back they can ensure it is mailed promptly. By moving the customer in question to ACH and promising to pay that day or the next, you will actually get the payment to the supplier faster than if they mailed the check.

Returning checks to requisitioners is an internal control issue that is likely to be with us as long as we are making payments using paper checks, another words, for a long time. Therefore it is incumbent upon those who work in or manage accounts payable that they find ways to ensure the internal controls embedded in that practice are as strong as possible.

Chapter 12: Corporate Procurement Cards:
An Alternative to Paper Checks

The Corporate Purchasing card is a means of streamlining the traditional purchase order and payment processes. Typically, it is used by organizations to pay for low-dollar purchases and is a way of getting all those small dollar invoices out of the accounts payable department. It is generally viewed as an attractive payment vehicle for organizations looking to lower transaction costs. These cards are also referred to as p-cards and corporate procurement cards. The IRS refers to them as payment cards.

Corporate Purchasing cards, also referred to as procurement cards or corporate procurement cards or p-cards, are similar to charge cards and operate very much like the credit card you have in your wallet. They are given to those employees who regularly make purchases on behalf of your organization. They should not automatically be given to all employees over a certain level, only those whose jobs require that they regularly make purchases on behalf of the company. In this section we explore:

- How the card should work, with a control mindset in place
- Fraud prevention
- Training

How the P-Card Process Should Work

There's no one set way that every best practice card program will operate. Corporate culture and unique organizational or industry requirements will impact the programs. However, some guidelines are appropriate. The National Association of Purchasing Card Professionals (NAPCP) recommends that:

- Plastic purchasing cards or non-plastic account numbers are issued to requisitioners.

- Each card/account is mapped to a general ledger (G/L) account. (In some cases G/L mapping can be done based on Merchant Category Codes or Point of Sale Information.)

- The requisitioner places orders with suppliers providing appropriate payment instructions.

- The supplier processes the order using their acquiring bank's authorization process.

- Cardholders receive their purchasing card statement directly from the card issuer. The cardholder reviews and approves the statement. Cardholders do not submit a payment.

- A single electronic invoice is sent from the card issuer to the requisitioner's organization on a monthly, weekly, or daily basis. The invoice is processed to create accounting entries and facilitate payment.

Individual Limits

One of the control features in the cards is the ability to set individual limits. Again, these should relate to job functionality and requirements not title. Some of the ways companies control p-card usage while simultaneously encouraging employees to use it wherever possible are:

- Limit the dollar amount of each transaction. Some companies set this limit as low as $50 or $100 to start and then when they become more comfortable with the program or want to grow it, they increase the limits. There are those who have limits as high as $5,000 and a few have no limits.

- Limit the dollar amount that each employee can spend in a given month. A repair person might be limited to no more than $1,000 per month while the plant supervisor might have a limit that is ten times that amount. Limits can be initially set low and then raised as needed. Remember, this level is not related to an individual's title.

- Use merchant category code (MCC) blocks. For example, some companies block furriers and other luxury goods stores. The problem with this issue is that sometimes companies are in more than one line of business, yet they are limited to one SIC code. There have been instances where employees have been blocked from making legitimate purchases. Only use these if you are concerned about inappropriate use.

- Insist that the manager review and sign off on all monthly statements. Remind managers that their signature makes them equally responsible for inappropriate charges.

Additionally, there should be a periodic review by someone independent of the cardholder.

Fraud Prevention

When p-cards first appeared on the scene there were some executives who refused to have the program in their shop because they were concerned that their employees would use the cards for personal purchases. Others, didn't go that far, but were extremely restrictive in who was given cards for basically the same reason. These fears were exaggerated. Yes, p-card fraud does occasionally occur, but then, so do other types of employee fraud.

Managers are urged to set up programs that have fraud protections built in. Some guidelines that will help include:

- Create a detailed cardholder agreement requiring the signature of the cardholder and the cardholder's supervisor. The agreement should contain a statement that the employee acknowledges the company's right to fire him if he uses the card inappropriately. Although the primary responsibility for using the card appropriately lies with the cardholder, the supervisor has the ultimate accountability for how the card is used. Should someone flagrantly misuse the card, his employment should be terminated and this fact should be made public. Unfortunately, sometimes it is necessary to set an example to show that you are serious about enforcing the policy.

- Create a detailed policies and procedures manual and update it regularly to reflect the p-card program roles and responsibilities accurately. This document can be put online so everyone who may need to access it can do so. The manual will not only spell out everyone's responsibilities it will provide the framework for the entire administrative process, including internal controls and fraud prevention.

- Appoint a permanent administrator responsible for the p-card program. The administrator will assure that all aspects of the card program are kept up to date and reflect the most current technology and management controls available. This person will also be responsible for training and retraining cardholders and transaction reconcilers, as well as monitoring for incidences of possible unintentional personal use or obvious misuse.

- If possible, design the card so employees won't accidentally mistake it for one of their own personal cards. If it looks like any other MasterCard, VISA or American Express it is an easy mistake to make. If your program is large enough, you may be able to get your logo put on the card. Recognize that honest mistakes do happen, but they occur very rarely.

- Establish reasonable card limits to reduce excessive or inappropriate use issues. Again, just because someone is a vice president, if their job does not require a $10,000 line, don't give it to them. There's no sense tempting fate. While 99 times out of 100, there will be no problem, why open the door to temptation.

- Require training before issuing a p-card to a new cardholder, and require refresher training at least every two years for continuing cardholders. The training can be face-to-face or computer/Web-based. Some organizations insist that it be face-to-face for new cardholders, but that is not always logistically possible.

- Require original receipts for all purchases made on the p-card. Every receipt doesn't have to be checked, but spot check and if you are at all suspicious, check all the receipts from the individual. Every photocopy increases the risk of fraud or abuse.

- Provide an anonymous hotline process to report suspected abuse. Every two years the Association of Certified Fraud Examiners (ACFE)produces a survey on Occupational Fraud entitled "Report to the Nation". In this report, the top ways fraud was uncovered were by an anonymous tip 34.2% of the time and by accident 25.4% of the time. Can you really afford *not* to have a tip line? Make sure you publicize this fact through your training.

- Have meaningful and enforced policies governing consequences for misuse. As discussed earlier, if intentional fraud is uncovered, the employee should be terminated. If it is possible, legal action should be pursued. This may seem harsh but it is important that your employees know there are consequences. The fraudster should be prosecuted, and the prosecution should be publicized. Not prosecuting and publicizing thefts only increases the chances that they will do it again.

- Establish a recurring audit process to evaluate compliance with program policies and requirements. Although routine monitoring is best handled by each operating unit's management, regular surprise audits of card usage will deter fraud significantly.
- Regularly review and update your policies and procedures as well as the limits on each card. This review does not necessarily mean that limits will be increased. If they are not being reached, they can and should be decreased.
- Don't overlook the ability to seasonally increase limits if your business requires such action. The limits can be lowered once the high season has passed.

Auditing the Program

Many organizations are concerned about fraud. Others want to ensure that all purchases that should be put on the card are because they want to receive as high a rebate as possible. This is not unusual and is becoming a larger issue.

Thus many will want to set up an audit program to see if p-cards are being used as they should be and in all instances where they are supposed to be.

The information gathered in these audits can be used by the purchasing personnel to help them negotiate better pricing from preferred vendors if all the activity is aggregated to one or two suppliers for large purchases of certain products.

End-User Training

Without adequate training, even the most carefully planned p-card program will have a hard time succeeding. This is an area that is often overlooked. People think that p-cards are just like credit cards and that they know how to use them so why do they need special training. While they are correct in the similarities with p-cards, they are incorrect in the assertion that they do not need any training.

Without training, the cards will be used for items that are not intended to be used for, reporting and monitoring of spending will be inaccurate and there will be clashes between the end users and the professionals responsible for monitoring the program.

The best training is onsite in-person instructions on how to use the cards and do the associated reporting. When the program is first rolled out, this is possible as there are usually a large number of employees who need to be trained. Unfortunately, onsite in-person training is often not possible for new hires or when employees are located in remote locations and there are only one or two in each branch using the card.

The next best training is given online, allowing each employee to take the training at his or her convenience. If possible, incorporate on-line testing to ensure that the employee has understood the material.

Some organizations go so far as to refuse to give a p-card to anyone who has not taken the training. As you might expect, you can anticipate some resistance, if not outright rebellion, to the last two recommendations.

Chapter 13: Electronic Payment Alternatives: A Better Payment Approach

Corporate America is *finally* starting to give up its paper-check security blanket. While wire transfers have long been used for high dollar payments, that mechanism is an expensive proposition. Financial Electronic Data Interchange (FEDI), once considered the reasonable alternative, has been adopted by only a handful of companies. If these were the only alternatives to the paper check, it is unlikely that we'd see the demise of even a small portion of the paper check market. But, they are not the only alternatives. In this section we investigate internal controls as they relate to:

- Wire transfers
- Electronic payments made via ACH
- Best electronic payment practices

Wire Transfers: Who's in Charge

Wire transfers may be a reasonable payment alternative when sending millions or even hundreds of thousands of dollars. The cost for a wire can be as high as $50, although typically it is somewhat lower. The first issue regarding wire transfers relates to where the responsibility for the function lies. This can be a serious consideration. In somewhere between 50 and 75% of all organizations the Treasury group does the wire transfers while checks are issued in accounts payable.

In those numerous instances where wire transfers are handled by a different group than those who are responsible for checks, there needs to be a coordination between the two groups.

Why? This is because in more instances than anyone would like to admit in public, many invoices that are paid with a wire are then paid again with a check. One of the ways this happens is that when a payment is late, the vendor will insist on a wire transfer. Then, when the original invoice finally does show up, it gets paid. One way to avoid this is when the vendor screams for a wire transfer, try and convince them to take an ACH payment. This will keep the payment in accounts payable, the cost down and hopefully reduce the risk of a duplicate payment.

More to the point, to tighten controls consider moving the responsibility for wire transfers to accounts payable, where other payments are originated.

Types

Wire transfers can be broken into two broad groups. The first are those that are made on a recurring basis and the second are those one time or irregularly made payments. This distinction is important when it comes to setting up wires online. It is also important when consideration is given to internal controls, fraud and duplicate payment prevention.

Initiating a Wire Transfer

Wire instructions can be sent to the bank online or by phone. Regardless of which initiation technique is used, the instructions need to be verified by a party other than the one that initiated the transaction. This is an important internal control point. It is especially important when it comes to preventing fraud. The list of people authorized to initiate wire transfers, as well as those authorized to approve the wires after they have been initiated should be limited to a small group of individuals. As with checks, this is not something that all executives should automatically have authority to do.

Now, when wires are done online, the process typically involves typing in the requisite information. Each approved person should have his or her own user ID and password. While it is not rocket scientist work, it is a task that involves some responsibility. Rarely is this task assigned to a clerical person – but that does not mean that in some organizations the clerical staff does not enter the data. Yes – that's right in some organizations the person who enters the data is not the one who is authorized to enter it.

Unfortunately, this can lead to fraud. Sharing passwords and user IDs is a really bad ideas. Now, before you start to explain that the person in your organization the person who's been entering the wires even though not authorized is a long-term trusted employee, consider this. Most employee fraud is committed by long-term trusted employees.

Fraud

It is not uncommon for a company to receive a call asking for wire instructions by someone looking to pay the company. Most of the time, these are legitimate requests. However, occasionally, they are not. Crooks have figured out that calling and asking for wire instructions claiming they are getting ready to pay a company is one of the easiest ways to get a company's bank account number. And what are you going to do – not give someone the wire instructions???

Thus, some companies use one account for wires and another for checks. If someone tries to write a check against the wire account it will bounce as the account cannot honor checks. This is not a Sarbanes-Oxley requirement but it is a good control point and could help you avoid getting dinged in the audit.

Automated Clearinghouse (ACH): Electronic Payments for the Masses

Americans' love affair with the paper check is finally abating. This is one area where the United States lags behind the rest of the world. In fact in many parts of the world checks are rarely written with most payments being made electronically.

There has been a seismic move in the corporate environs

toward making payments via the Automated Clearinghouse (ACH), mostly through the use of ACH credits, and in limited instances through a debit vehicle referred to as an ACH debit. If you are planning on skipping the sections on ACH because your firm is not currently initiating payments through that mechanism, reconsider that idea. For starters there are types of ACH fraud that everyone, regardless of whether they actually use ACH, can be hit with. Then there is the issue that even companies who have no plans to use ACH suddenly find themselves making payments that way when a large supplier demands electronic payments.

A reasonable number of organizations are making payments or are considering making payments in the near term using the ACH. The most common examples of ACH payments are direct deposit of payroll and of social security payments. These are what are referred to as ACH credits. If you allow your bank to automatically deduct your monthly mortgage payment from your bank account, you are using ACH debits.

This type of payment is infinitely more affordable than wire transfers. At approximately ten cents per item, ACH payments are even cheaper than paper checks. To be perfectly honest, ACH have fewer control problems associated with them. There is no concern about employees in the mailroom snatching the payments, payments don't get lost in the mail, and so on.

Authorization

In order to pay vendors electronically, it is necessary to have them sign up. Care needs to be taken with the forms that vendors fill out with all their secure information. It should not be kept where anyone can stumble across it. Treat it as though it were your own bank information.

Most companies once they start making payments using the ACH want to expand their programs. From a control standpoint it is important that all payment mechanisms (e.g., checks, wires, and ACH) are coordinated so that duplicate payments are not made and that weaknesses are introduced into the processes that will allow fraud.

One of the good things about the ACH payment mechanism is that because it is relatively new in most organizations, the controls surrounding them are usually good. Typically, but not always, because there is generally some reluctance to start paying electronically, a company will have instituted decent internal controls around the process.

Positive Pay

Care needs to be taken when paying electronically. The reason for this is that positive pay does not work with ACH payments. While there is talk about developing a product, one is not currently available. Remember, ACH can work as either a credit or a debit. While ACH fraud is not nearly as prevalent as check fraud, it does exist and you need to protect against it. So, as a rule of thumb, unless you allow ACH debits, you can put an ACH block on your accounts.

There are other products available from banks to protect an organization against ACH fraud. Combined with strong internal controls they provide a framework for an integrated fraud-resistant payment process.

Protecting Your Bank Accounts

Whether you make electronic payments or not, you can use the following tools to protect your accounts.

- **ACH Blocks.** ACH blocks are the simplest of all the products to use. They allow companies to notify their banks that ACH debits should not be allowed on certain accounts. With a block in place, no ACH debit, even one that is authorized, will be able to get through on a given account. Everyone is advised to put blocks in place on all accounts where ACH activity is not likely to be used.

- **ACH Filters.** An ACH filter allows organizations to give their banks a list of companies authorized to debit their accounts. The banks will then "filter" incoming debits and allow through only those that are on the list submitted earlier. This filter does not check for dollar amounts or whether the particular transaction has been authorized, only that the company doing the debiting is on the approved list.

More Electronic Payment Fraud Prevention Tips

While you can't stop someone from trying to steal from your organization, you can make it so difficult they are not successful. What follows is a list of tactics any organization can use to prevent a fraudster from winning when trying to steal from your firm using the ACH.

1. Set up a separate computer for online banking activity only.

2. Put ACH blocks on all accounts where ACH activity is not to be initiated; if you are paying using ACH credits, put ACH debit blocks on your accounts.

3. Put ACH filters on accounts where ACH debit activity is permitted.

4. Set up a single account for incoming wire transfers, allowing no other activity in that account. Sweep it each night into another account.

5. Do not give wire transfer information over the phone.

6. Issue refund checks from a separate account with a low-dollar limit.

7. Regular update of security and anti-virus software.

8. Do not automatically reply to messages; retype the address in to prevent yourself from inadvertently replying to spoofed messages.

Detection

Sometimes, no matter how hard you try, an unauthorized transaction gets through. If that happens, all is not lost. If you notify the bank within 24 hours, they can retrieve your money. The following strategies are recommended for detecting unauthorized activity.

1. Perform daily bank reconciliations to identify unauthorized activity.
2. Notify the bank immediately of unauthorized activity.

Recurring Payments

The ACH can be used automatically, as with checks, to make recurring payments (e.g., mortgage, rent, lease, loan payments, etc.) As with checks, it is a good control point to set these payments up with a maturity date so they do not go on after the maturity of the obligation. Additionally it is a good idea to periodically review recurring payments to make sure that none should have been terminated. This might happen if a loan is prepaid or the interest rate renegotiated or if a property is sold thus ending a mortgage obligation.

Some companies review their list of recurring payments each month before they are made to ensure that all the obligations are still outstanding.

Daily Reconciliations

It is a very good idea to reconcile bank accounts daily when it comes to ACH payments. This should be done for several reasons. Since positive pay doesn't work with ACH payments, the protection offered by that product is not available. Additionally, corporations have a very short time frame to dispute incorrect or invalid items. Thus from an internal control standpoint – whether you use the ACH mechanism or not – the frequent checking and verification are important.

Those firms that have not put ACH blocks on their accounts, daily bank reconciliations are mandatory if they do not want to end up holding an empty bag. For they have only 24 hours to notify their bank of an unauthorized transaction. Waiting until the end of the month simply doesn't work anymore.

The Electronic Control Best Practice Checklist

Best Practice #1: Have detailed written procedures for your ACH program and include them in the accounts payable policy and procedures manual.

Best Practice #2: Make sure your ACH procedures mirror you check procedures.

Best Practice #3: Integrate strong internal controls throughout the process.

Best Practice #4: Check for duplicate payments made using other payment methodologies, i.e. paper check, T&E and p-card. Ideally every organization should be paid using one and only one payment mechanism.

Best Practice #5: Make sure receivers and POs are extinguished just as they would be if a paper check was the payment mechanism.

Best Practice #6: Put ACH blocks on all accounts where ACH activity will not be allowed. This is something every organization should do, regardless of its participation in the electronic payment arena.

Best Practice #7: Use ACH filters on those accounts where ACH debit activity will be allowed.

Best Practice #8: Have daily bank account reconciliations done on all accounts where ACH debits are permitted. Even better, reconcile all bank accounts on a daily basis.

Best Practice #9: Use a separate PC for all your online banking activities and do not use it for anything else.

Best Practice #10: Keep up to date on the latest information regarding fraud protection products offered by your financial institution and new frauds being perpetrated by crooks. They are getting amazingly creative.

Closing Thoughts

The ACH payment mechanism is rapidly gaining acceptance. As check fraud remains a big problem, the efficiencies it introduces into the process are undeniable and it is actually the least expensive payment alternative available. Even if your firm is able to dismiss these considerations, a number of vendors are demanding that their customers pay them electronically as part of their contract. Thus, most experts believe it is only a matter of time before every company will be making payments electronically.

Many banks already have products that allow consumers to make electronic payments and some are developing similar products for small businesses. The fact that the process is new means that accounts payable will not have to live with antiquated policies and procedures that are full of weaknesses and internal control points.

If your company decides to introduce an electronic process, and it probably will if one is not currently in use, take the opportunity to make sure that no weaknesses are permitted. Develop strong procedures that have the appropriate checks and balances and control points built in.

Additionally, the processes for the ACH need to be integrated into the entire payment process and tie into good control points. As new technology emerges expect more changes and improvements to the electronic payment world.

Chapter 14: Master Vendor File: Where it All Begins

The master vendor file is the repository of information related to the vendor and is used to make payments. That is part of the reason it is critical that strong controls be implemented around the master vendor file. It is also one of the reasons why access to the file for purposes of adding vendors or changing information about existing vendors should be severely restricted. In this section we'll take a look at:

- Common practices (good and bad) around vendor set ups
- Controls around the master vendor file
- Naming Conventions
- Segregation of Duties

When Should the Vendor Be Set Up in the Master Vendor File?

Many believe that vendor issues are the sole province of the purchasing department. While procurement has the primary association with the vendor, there is an equally important connection with accounts payable. If the road between accounts payable and the vendor is rocky, everyone suffers. A vendor who doesn't get paid promptly may decide to put the organization on credit hold. Even if that does not occur, there can be delay in shipments, time wasted unnecessarily as the vendor and accounts payable try and resolve discrepant invoices, and if matters aren't handled properly, duplicate payments that are not returned.

Therefore it is my contention that the sooner the accounts

payable function is alerted to a new relationship with a vendor; the better it will be for both the supplier and the customer. They can begin to collect information, do whatever verification is needed and will be discussed further in this work and be ready to pay when the first invoice shows up. Unfortunately, what happens most frequently is the first time accounts payable learns about the new vendor is when the invoice shows up. Then one of several scenarios plays out.

New Vendor Set-up Spectrum

How vendors are set up in the master vendor file is most definitely an internal control issue. Unfortunately not everyone realizes that. How this function is handled varies widely. Let's look at several representative situations.

The Complete Lack of Control Scenario

The processor gets the invoice and looks in the master vendor file to try and find the vendor. Not finding it, he or she sets up the vendor using the information on the invoice and proceeds to process the invoice. They may or may not have been correct in their assumption that the vendor wasn't in the master vendor file. They may simply have spelled the name incorrectly or someone else had entered the vendor maybe using its DBA or some other similar name. In this scenario, the processor may make a cursory attempt to determine if a 1099 will have to be issued. If they decide one will be needed, they may mail or e-mail the vendor asking for a W-9. Maybe the vendor provides one or equally possible, the vendor simply discards the request. No tracking is done to ensure the W-9 is returned.

It will probably come as no surprise to most reading this to learn that this approach completely negates the requisite segregation of duties required in the accounts payable function. It is also likely duplicate payments will slip through. Finally, there's a decent chance that the correct information reporting at tax time will not be done.

It should also be noted that this lackadaisical approach to setting up vendors in the master vendor file is likely to allow fraudulent invoices to not only get through, but the crooked vendors could end up in the master vendor file. That way, when the crook emboldened by his or her success with the first invoice sends a second larger invoice, there's a good chance the invoice will be paid.

Keep in mind, the scenario here is being presented as a worst case. Most organizations, even if they don't have the controls they should around the master vendor file and a process in place for new vendors do rely on the three-way match and purchaser approvals to avoid the complete disaster described here. However, also keep in mind that many purchasers routinely approve invoices without giving too much attention to the details.

The Average Control Scenario

In this situation, the processor gets the invoice realizes it is not in the master vendor file and stops processing. The invoice is sent over to the person responsible for the master vendor file and he or she sets up the vendor. This is an improvement over the earlier case as at least there is some semblance of segregation of duties used.

Regrettably, if the best practices regarding data entry discussed later in this work are not used, this situation is only marginally improved over the earlier one. It is still possible to get vendors in the master vendor file more than once and if no attempt is made to solicit taxpayer identification number information, information reporting at tax time is likely to be inaccurate.

The Tight Control Scenario

In this situation, the procurement professional notifies accounts payable the moment they are considering doing business with a new vendor, before the first purchase order is written. The person responsible for new vendor setup, immediately contacts the vendor with the organization's vendor application or profile form. As part of this process, a W-9 is sent to collect the necessary taxpayer number information. And, if the vendor is deemed to be critical, credit information is also gathered to be analyzed, again before the purchase order is submitted.

Once the vendor returns all the information, the person responsible for the master vendor file sets the vendor up using all the best practices discussed later in the work. The taxpayer identification number is run through TIN Matching and assuming everything matches, the vendor is good to go. If there is a mismatch, the vendor is contacted to get the information corrected.

Only after the company has all the information needed is the company permitted to issue the first purchase order. An organization that follows these guidelines is also likely to employ good practices throughout their accounts payable function thus minimizing the number of duplicate payments and almost eliminating fraudulent invoices that make it through the process.

What's more, a company that explains to the vendor exactly what its processes are and how it operates on the payment side is likely to run into few problems with its vendors. For, let's be honest, all any vendor really wants is for your organization to place lots of orders with it and to pay them on time.

You can probably guess that the best case scenario for your organization is the last setting presented. Are you there yet?

Master Vendor File Controls

How good your master vendor file is will depend on many factors. How strong it is will depend on the internal controls you employ around the process. But, the data in the file is critical and how it is handled will make a big difference in the protections the file affords the organization. Let's take a look at some of them.

Best Practice Overview

Why would you want to use best practices? If you employ best practices it will make cleaning up the master vendor file easier while helping tighten controls and reduce duplicate payments. Not all duplicate payments, but duplicate payments associated with having a vendor in the Master Vendor File more than once. It will make employee fraud more difficult, and unfortunately, every organization at one time or another is going to have to deal with employee fraud. It happens. It doesn't happen a lot, but it does happen. And, as discussed earlier, if you start collecting W9s and tracking them, information reporting will get easier, and you'll also increase your SOX compliance if you're a public company.

Every organization must have strong internal controls to be in compliance with the *Sarbanes-Oxley Act.* If an organization has poor master vendor file practices, it doesn't have good strong internal controls. Master vendor file is just another one of those features, another part of the process, and you do need to have strong controls.

Best Practice: Controls

For starters everyone needs to limit access to the master vendor file. This is both for updating the master vendor file and adding new vendors. Now too often what happens, is that the associates are processing invoices, and everything is going along fine, and then he/she looks to input an invoice and they can't find the vendor in the master vendor file. They say, "Wait a second. Hold on. I've got to enter this vendor in the master vendor file." They go ahead and update it. That is a poor way to handle this problem.

What that means is that anybody can go in and update, or anybody with processing access and that is not an appropriate segregation of duties. With segregation of duties, we want to have one person doing each leg of the transaction. That means somebody approving invoices, somebody entering them, someone entering data in the master vendor file, someone printing checks if you're paying by checks, and someone signing checks—all handled by different employees.

Sometimes, if you only have one or two people with access to the master vendor file, and they're taking vacations, they might be tempted to give their passwords to somebody else so they can do it in their absence. Resist that temptation. A much better strategy is to give that person their own password for the time in question while the original person is on vacation and then close off that access when the person comes back. Sharing passwords is just not a good idea.

Naming Conventions: Increase Control

Sometimes naming conventions are referred to as coding standards. They should address every last possible issue that your processes might have when entering data. There's nothing too small or too miniscule about it. Even if something as simple as addresses, for example, if you think that street should be abbreviated ST. You may have somebody who thinks it's STR. There's nothing wrong with doing it either way as long as everybody does it the same.

A simple tip when you're trying to decide what to put in your standard, for address purposes use the standard set by the US Post Office.

More about the Naming Convention

There are many issues to address when creating your naming convention. Remember, for most items there is no right or wrong way. The important issue is that every processor enters the data using the same standard. Here are a few of the more common issues to consider.

Issue #1: Punctuation. What do you do when there's a comma? John Jones, Jr or John Jones Jr.

Issue #2: Spaces and Abbreviations. This is especially important. Spaces and abbreviations can create monster problems. What do you do for IBM? Does it go in as IBM, I B M? Does it go with International Business Machines? There are many varieties of that, as you can see. Decide what you think is best and then set it in stone for everyone entering information. Sometimes there's punctuation in a vendors' names. Do you include it? When you put Wendy's in for example, if you're doing business with the hamburger chain, do you put the apostrophe in? If you put it in and someone else doesn't put it in, it won't look like a match. You want to have a list of abbreviations. Again, do you put in corp.? Do you spell out corporation? Do you put Corp or Corp with a period after it? You want to address all these issues.

Issue #3: The Doing-Business-As (DBA) Issue. You want to make sure you avoid DBA's. Insist on the use of the company's legal name.

Issue #4: Leading Articles. When it comes to leading articles, do you include them or not? Do you put 'The Gap' in or do you put 'Gap' in? Again, there is no right or wrong way, just as long as everybody does it exactly the same.

Issue #5: Individual's Names. When you put individual's names in, and you will if you're using independent contractors, consultants, you'll find that you have a number of them. Which do you put in first name: the first name or last name? Do you put in Mary Schaeffer or Schaeffer Mary? Again, there is no right or wrong way as long as everyone does it the same.

Issue #6 Titles. Do you want to include titles? Mr., Ms., Dr., III, Jr., Sr. etc. What about professional designations after someone's name: CPA, PhD, and things like that. Also, what do you want to do with middle initials? Include them or not include them? While it's not a definite best practice, it's probably a good idea to include them, especially in a large organization. When you have people with common names, sometimes middle initials are what can save you. It's not unusual to have two Jack Smiths, especially if you're a large company. Having the middle initial will help you distinguish one from the other.

Issue #7: Industry Specific Issues. You also might want to consider any unique issues that you might have that are peculiar to your industry. The best one that comes to mind are vendors who change their name annually. You may be thinking, "What is she talking about change their name annually?" The one that comes to my mind is the US Tennis Open in New York. Its official name changes each year. One year it will be the 2013 US Tennis Open, and next year it will be the 2014 US Tennis Open. What do you do about that? How do you address that issue?

Most people don't give much thought to the contact information in their master vendor file. This is unfortunate. What's worse, is the contact information is often that of the sales person at your supplier. While this may be fine if you want to place another order, and that is what the sales person is hoping, the information is useless for most accounts payable inquiries. As you will see, it is critical that good contact information be maintained.

Vendor Contact Information

We've alluded to the need for good contact information because of some emerging issues that are going on and why we now have an additional challenge in accounts payable. Specifically, you need to be ready in case you are hit with ACH fraud, which you may refer to as electronic payment fraud. The crooks involved in this generally are very sophisticated and their technology skills far exceed mine and probably many reading this today. Unfortunately, this puts a new onus on accounts payable.

Change of Bank Account Requests

When you get those change-of-bank account requests from your vendors or what looks to be like your vendors, you need to verify that these changes came from a legitimate party. To accomplish this, you need to have that good contact information in your master vendor file. The requests typically are coming by email, but they may come in a letter on company letterhead. Whichever way they come they look legitimate. I got one myself from what reported to be Chase

Manhattan Bank. It looked like a legitimate email. The email even looked like it came from Chase Manhattan Bank. The only way I was sure it was a fraud was the fact that I don't have an account with Chase Manhattan bank.

When these requests arrive, you certainly can't respond to the email that was sent, and you certainly can't call the phone number that the supposed vendor has very considerately provided in the email. Because of course if you call that phone number or respond to the email, they're going to verify the faulty information. They're going to say that the change is a legitimate transaction. Therefore you need to have that updated contact information somewhere, but ideally in the master vendor file, otherwise potentially, you will have a big problem.

How Good Is Your Contact Information?

Let's consider a few issues. When was the last time you cleansed your contact information in your master vendor file or wherever you have it? If you're like most of your peers reading this, your organization has never updated it. Most companies just don't do this. Now, we shared some statistics at the beginning of this work about changes and how often people change jobs. Consider this. How good do you think your contact information is?

Is there a better way? Ideally, when you first set up the vendor, get contact information, get the information for somebody in accounts receivable or treasury that you can call when you have a problem. Once this information is obtained, store it somewhere safe with ready access for all who might need it. One place might be in the master vendor file. If you don't have room there, you can keep it elsewhere, but keep it, and then regularly update that information. Now sometimes, people will say, "We're overloaded as it is. How do you think we're going to take that on? We can't take that on," and it is a legitimate issue. But so is having ready access when you need it. There are now companies who outsource this. You can outsource this function and the outsourcer will collect this data for you.

The other approach that a small but growing number of companies are starting to use is to create an online portal or an online master vendor file where the vendor is responsible for inputting and updating the information. Perhaps once a quarter or once a year, you could send an email that says, "Has any of your information changed? If it has, please go to the vendor portal and update it." This is a simple approach that gets vendors to update their information. Then, you've got the good information you need when you have to verify those phony requests that unfortunately have a way of trickling in.

The accounts payable function is changing. It's rapidly evolving. As you can see, from a lot of the stuff that we talked about with the master vendor file, how we can treat our vendor data is changing. What we all need to do is make sure our practices are up to date, that we revamp them, that we continue to look at them and make sure that they meet the changing business requirements that we need.

Fraud through the Master Vendor File

Not all vendor fraud is external. We've mentioned fraud using the master vendor file several times now and you may be wondering how this can be done. Needless to say, your employees with larceny in their hearts can probably find more ways to play games than we can identify. We'll hone in on a few of the easier scams.

The most common vendor master file game is to simply submit a phony invoice (usually for a small dollar amount) for payment. If your controls are weak and someone approves the phony invoice because they are rushed, the vendor has then attained "legitimacy" and then future phony invoices, perhaps for larger dollar amounts, can slip through.

More devious employees have been known to hone in on inactive vendors that are still live in the master vendor file.

They then submit an invoice under that vendor's name and address. Now, here comes the tricky part. Once the invoice has been approved for payment, the thieving employee goes into the master vendor file and changes the Remit To address to their own address or that of an accomplice. Once they have the check in hand, they go back to the master vendor file and change the Remit To address back to the original address.

These same tricks can be used to divert payments from a legitimate vendor to your dishonest employee.

In Closing: A Word about Segregation of Duties

The backbone of all internal controls is a good segregation of duties. This is not to be ignored when discussing the master vendor file. Those who have the ability to make changes to existing vendor information or to add new vendors should not be able to perform any other leg in the procure-to-pay function.

Without a doubt, this is where segregation of duties constraints sometimes starts to fray. As technology starts to play a larger role in the way the accounts payable function is handled, the departments will get smaller. This could place additional pressures on segregating duties in an appropriate and applicable manner.

Chapter 15: The Travel and Entertainment Component: Expense Reimbursements

When the topic of internal controls in accounts payable is considered, few remember to include expense reimbursements in the discussion. This is unfortunate because loose controls in the expense reimbursement process usually have a negative impact on the organization's bottom line. Loose controls sometimes result in duplicate reimbursements or reimbursements for dubious charges. And unfortunately, honest mistakes sometimes trigger additional frauds when the recipient realizes the loose controls make it possible to play games.

In this section, we'll look at:

- The Importance of a Strong Expense Reimbursement Policy
- The Importance of Uniform Enforcement of the Policy
- Real Life examples of where policies sometimes fall apart
- Tactics to tighten controls and stop expense reimbursement fraud

The Expense Reimbursement Policy

First, it goes without saying, that every organization should have a written T&E policy. It should be given to every employee who either travels or handles any T&E matters, including filling out reimbursement requests for superiors. Ideally, the policy (and all updates) should be in the hands of any traveler, *before* they travel.

The policy should be updated every time there is a change and reviewed at least once a year. More frequently is fine; less frequently can lead to trouble.

The policy should be posted for everyone to see. There should be no secrets so there is no reason to limit access. Posting on the company Intranet site eliminates all sorts of problems and the no-one-told-me-that excuse.

New employees should be given a copy of the T&E policy as part of their welcome packet.

In theory, when an expense account report and reimbursement request is sent down to accounts payable approved by the appropriate manager, accounts payable should merely pay the reimbursement. Unfortunately in many organizations, policy compliance falls on the shoulders of the accounts payable group although they don't have any real authority to enforce it. Talk about an oxymoron.

The reality is that few managers actually check the T&E reports submitted by their subordinates. They merely approve whatever is put in front of them. The reasons for this are numerous and largely irrelevant to this discussion. The bottom line is that most expense reports are not checked or verified by the person who puts their signature on the approval line.

The policy should contain statements about managerial responsibility and a decision should be made internally about whether accounts payable is expected to check for policy compliance. Most companies do want their accounts payable group to check for policy compliance because they recognize that their managers are not doing it. If you make that decision, make sure that you back the managers who enforce the policy—because they are anything but popular when they do it.

Of course, an easy way around this issue is to use one of the nifty models on the market today that incorporate a policy compliance feature. Many of these refuse to let employees enter an item that is outside the policy. This takes the onus off both the approving manager and the accounts payable staff. However, at this juncture, many companies are still relying on their staff to check for policy compliance.

The Importance of Uniform Enforcement of the Policy

It also goes without saying that the policy should be administered uniformly. Managers should not be allowed to okay policy violations. Not only is that not fair to other employees, it could get you into trouble in your S-Ox audit and, in extreme situations, with the IRS. The latter could occur if an ineligible payment was made.

For a T&E policy to be effective, it has to be enforced across the board. This means that managers should not be allowed to override the policy, where they think it does not apply to their staff. Obviously, for the policy to be effective it also needs to be adhered to by executives at all levels.

Policy enforcement should not fall on the shoulders of the Accounts Payable (AP) department. That really is not fair. Companies using an automated system can have a policy compliance feature built in. In these systems, reports that are in violation of the company policy are flagged for further investigation. The AP department can then return these reports to the approver's supervisor for further review.

Some of the more advanced automated systems take policy compliance one step further. They refuse to allow the submission of reports in violation of the policy. This is a bit extreme, as there will infrequently be occasions when an expense outside the policy is justified.

Ideally, there should be a focal point for questions relating to the T&E policy.

Frequent T&E policy violators should be noted and their reports checked thoroughly each time one is submitted.

Senior management must support the policy in a very public way. Some companies do this effectively by having either the chief executive officer (CEO) or the chief financial officer (CFO) sign the cover memo that goes out with the policy. Others do it by having one of these senior officials sign a memo about T&E policy compliance that is put in the front of the T&E policy manual.

Where Policies Sometimes Fall Apart

No one likes to think about it or admit it could happen to them. But, the harsh fact is it will happen at most organizations and in many cases more than once. I'm talking about employees stealing from their employer and most specifically, employees using their travel and entertainment (T&E) to do it. In a recent survey by the *Accounts Payable Now & Tomorrow* newsletter, almost 40% of the respondents indicated they had witnessed T&E fraud in their organizations. The Association of Certified Fraud Examiners (ACFE) reports that almost 20% of all frauds committed by employees are expense reimbursement fraud. And, we're not talking about small dollar stuff, like a movie charged to a hotel bill or a glass of wine on a restaurant bill when alcohol is expressly forbidden by the policy. The average loss related to T&E, according to the ACFE is $25,000.

Now, if that does not seem like a huge amount of money, consider this common real-life scenario. Many larger frauds were first uncovered when a T&E fraud was investigated and it turned out an employee stealing in other ways from the organization could not resist the temptation to cheat on his or her expense report. Some of the stories are ingenious, although to be honest, some of the crooks are just down right stupid. Let's take a look at some real life stories and then focus on the controls and best practices that will prevent this from happening in your organization. But before we do, I want to share one more chilling fact with you. Most frauds are committed by long term trusted employees, not newcomers.

Dual Reimbursements

An employee with a corporate purchasing card did not turn in all his receipts on his purchasing log but would instead submit them on his T&E. The company thus paid the expenses twice. Variations on this fraud include getting reimbursed from the company petty cash box or requesting a check be sent to the vendor through the accounts payable process, while asking for reimbursement on the T&E expense report.

This type of fraud can be thwarted by establishing a strict schedule of which vendors are paid by p-cards, which are paid by check and which should be submitted on a T&E expense reimbursement request. Of course, if an issue had been made of the missing receipts, the fraud might have stopped.

Any unusual requests for reimbursement on the T&E report should be thoroughly investigated. Even if the fraud is not uncovered, it may serve as a deterrent against future frauds of this type with this particular employee. If the processor is suspicious about a particular request, check the vendor file to see if the vendor has already been paid.

This particular fraud was discovered, as many are, by accident.

Going the *Extra* Mile

A traveling salesman routinely added miles to his T&E reimbursement request. The accounts payable manager became suspicious and pulled out a year's worth of reports, tracked his routes and discovered he had put in for and been reimbursed an extra $1400 over the course of one year. This type of petty fraud happens more frequently than you might imagine.

Mileage can be estimated using online sites, like Mapquest, offering driving directions. While it is not recommended that ever trip be checked this way, processors should spot check the mileage requests of their travelers requesting reimbursement for miles driven. Additionally, the manager who approved this salesperson's expense reports was probably in the best position to uncover and stop the fraud. However, an ongoing issue for many organizations is the lackadaisical approach many managers take to approving employees' expense reimbursement requests. Holding them accountable for frauds might make them more attentive to the issue.

Some reading this may think this is petty theft. And, they are correct. However, people who get away with this type of fraud tend to escalate their thievery over time.

Airline Pricing Opportunities

Airlines and their complex pricing policies create a whole set of headaches for those checking T&E or many opportunities for those looking to pad their expense reports. This particular fraud only works if you do not insist that employees use company credit cards to book their corporate travel. While many employees honestly search for the very best price for their business trips, some also search for the very worst – and then book both flights. They take the cheapie flight but request reimbursement using the receipt they received when booking the more expensive flight – which they get a refund for.

Since the company doesn't see the employees personal credit card statement, it never sees the refund. This is just one of the reasons corporate credit cards are a good idea. The boarding pass, which could be used in old days to verify which flight was taken, can be easily altered by those with just a modicum of computer skills. Therefore, requiring boarding passes no longer provides the protection it once did.

Fine Dining—Not!

The question of when to require receipts is often hotly debated. If you require receipts for everything over a small dollar level, your processors will be inundated with small pieces of paper for small dollar amounts. However, you could have employees who submit requests for meals never eaten, right under the dollar threshold where receipts are required. One company had an employee who requested reimbursement of $12,000 over a three year period for bogus meals.

The employee in question took his theft one step further. He was caught because he got sloppy with his receipts, which were numbered. He began to submit them in numeric order. Organizations are advised to look at 14 months of T&E reports for a certain number of employees each year as an audit. Frauds such as this one jump out when the reports are reviewed in totality, while they might not be so apparent when reviewed separately. Again, if the approver had been more diligent, this fraud might have been stopped earlier on.

The Receipt Debate

While the IRS requires receipts for anything over $75, most organizations have not followed suit, with the most common threshold being $25. The most perplexing issue for some organizations is the preponderance of reimbursement requests right below the dollar threshold where receipts are required. There are two sides to this issue. The first believes that if an employee on a legitimate business trip puts in for $24.95 reimbursement when in actuality he ate a peanut butter sandwich in his room that is fraud and bad for the organization.

The second group says, 'hey, if we insist on a receipt, he'll go out for an $80 meal which is a lot more than the $25 we gave him for the peanut butter sandwich." They believe everyone is better off.

Best Practices to Deter & Detect T&E Fraud

1. Have a comprehensive written, easily accessible T&E policy that describes what is allowed and what is not in as much detail as possible. Don't leave anything open to employee good sense. Everyone has a few that are seriously lacking in that arena.

2. Enforce the policy 100% across the board. Do not have any exceptions. It leads to poor morale, and encourages other employees to emulate the success of the non-

conformers. Finally, it could create HR situations where you cannot terminate an employee who violates the rules as it could be deemed discriminatory.

3. Let your employees know that you have a zero tolerance for policy abuse. This should come from the top, ideally in a letter from the CEO, CFO or other high level executive. It should be the first page of the policy.

4. Give the processors the right to question any item that looks suspicious.

5. Make approvers understand that they are responsible for what they approve and could be considered a co-conspirator if they sign off on a expense request that has obviously fraudulent activity.

6. Require the use of a company credit card with no personal expenses allowed on the card. Copies of the card statements should come to the company each month for review.

7. At least once a year review and update your policy.

Concluding Thoughts

Expect T&E fraud. It is a fact of business life. Let your employees know it won't be tolerated. If you are thinking it is just not worth all the trouble, consider this.

Many larger frauds were only uncovered after a T&E fraud was discovered. In the course of investigating the T&E fraud, the larger frauds were uncovered. Many successful crooks cannot resist dipping into the company pot one more time when they submit their T&E expense report. Take advantage of their greed.

Additional Tactics that Tighten Controls around Expense Reimbursements

The following will tighten controls, prevent inappropriate spending and stop fraud through the expense reimbursement process:

Tactic #1 Have a detailed written travel and

entertainment policy. It should spell out what is expected as well as what the organization will reimburse the employee for. If there are some items that will not be reimbursed, this should be spelled out as well. The most common of these is liquor, if the organization does not reimburse for it. This is an area where assuming your employees have common sense will cause problems. Don't leave anything up to their discretion. You will quickly find that you have one or more employees severely lacking in this arena.

Your policy will only protect the organization if you incorporate consequences for not adhering to the policy. If you don't your policy will not do the job you want it to do. And, the more employees are able to push items through that should not be reimbursed, the more this problem will grow as they share their "successes" with each other.

Tactic #2 Insist on use of a corporate card for all business travel. Without going through all the different smarmy games employees can play when they use personal credit cards, suffice it to say that by insisting on the corporate card, you stop those games before they have a chance to get off the ground.

If employees insist on using personal cards, even after being given a company card, take action. Warn them that the next time, they will not be reimbursed and then stick to your guns, if they use their personal card after receiving the warning.

Tactic #3 Require the detailed meal receipt as well as a receipt for every item where reimbursement is requested. Again, this eliminates many of the games employees play with their expense reports. The detailed meal receipt lets you monitor the liquor issue as well as how many people actually attended the meal. The receipt for every expenditure requirement eliminates the games that more than a few play requesting reimbursement just below the receipt level.

We should be clear that just because we recommend you collect all the receipts, we are not advocating you check every last receipt, unless you uncover a problem. Continue using the spot checking approach that you utilize for all receipts, including the meal receipts in your verification process.

Tactic #4 Make managers responsible for the expense reimbursement reports they approve. Too many of the expense reimbursement shenanigans and frauds occur because the employee knows from experience that his or her manager is not going to review the expense report. They've seen the manager take the report and sign on the approved line without ever looking at the report. They bank on this behavior to ensure their games will fly under the radar.

Just telling the manager that he or she should review the expense report before approving it is likely to make little impact or change this behavior. In order for that to happen there has to be consequences for the failure to review. While one or two organizations have gone so far as to incorporate firing for the manager as well as the employee as the consequence for failure to review should a completely inappropriate approved expenditure surface, most organizations are not willing to take this step for simply failing to review the expense report. However, including this as an item in the annual review, and perhaps reducing the annual increase of any manager found approving an expense report with items on it that were obviously inappropriate or fraudulent is a step some are willing to take.

Tactic #5 Enforce the travel and reimbursement policy uniformly. This relatively simple approach will save you much aggravation. However, getting management's backing may not be as easy as it sounds. In a recent survey by the *Accounts Payable Now & Tomorrow* newsletter of its readers, 80% reported uniform enforcement of their policy. Alas, this means 20% were not enforcing it uniformly across the board.

The problem with uneven enforcement of the policy is two-fold. First, there is the obvious financial loss due to the excessive expenditure approved for payment. This is money that comes right out of the organization's profit, dollar for dollar. But there is another issue, more insidious, that is often ignored. Uneven enforcement encourages other employees to emulate the behavior of those playing games. They think, "Well if so-and-so can put in for whatever, why can't I?" What's more, these creative expense items tend to get larger over time. The Association of Certified Fraud Examiners report that most expense reimbursement frauds go on for two years. So, while each individual amount may not be large, the amounts attributable to items that should not have been included can add up.

Reimbursing employees for legitimate business expenses as spelled out in the travel and entertainment policy is what accounts payable (or the travel and entertainment group) is supposed to do. That is their responsibility. The reason for their review is to uncover items that should not be reimbursed. By employing the tactics discussed above, you will be on the road to achieving that mission. What's more, you will not have to wonder whether the employee tried to mislead you on purpose or simply didn't know any better. The strategies discussed should help tighten controls and stop fraud dead in its tracks.

Chapter 16: Computers, Tablets and Smartphones: The Often-Overlooked Control Component

An ever-growing number of professionals are stepping up their personal technology game through the use of smartphones and tablets. They are purchasing these devices with their own funds. In addition to using them for personal matters, some dedicated employees are bringing them to work to improve their workplace efficiency. And, that is where one of the newest issues facing accounts payable lies. Unless this matter is addressed adequately, these employees are unintentionally weakening internal controls and introducing additional risk into the payment and data stream of the organization.

In this piece we take a look at:

- What the BYOD issue is
- How it affects the accounts payable function
- How to design a company-wide policy to minimize risk

There is a seismic change occurring in the workplace and it's impacting the accounts payable function in ways never imagined before. With roots in the consumer arena, this particular technology issue is forcing organizations everywhere to reevaluate the very core of their processes, procedures and policies. We're talking about the BYOD movement, which is impacting a great number of organizations.

What is BYOD?

BYOD stands for Bring Your Own Device, and in this context, device refers to smartphone or tablet. Some include laptops in that definition. When Apple introduced the ipad in April 2010, not many saw it having anything to do with accounts payable in the foreseeable future. We've come a long way in a very short period of time. It is estimated that 250 million tablets will be sold in 2013.

In the past, virtually all hardware used by professionals in the course of their jobs was purchased by their employers. This gave the company control over security issues and, to some limited extent; control over what their employees did with that hardware. With the introduction of affordable tablets and smartphones that is changing. Individuals are purchasing these devices in droves for their personal use and then utilizing them for work purposes as well. This makes them more productive and gives them greater flexibility.

The use of personal devices for business purposes has been going on for a few years now. The first reports we had were of managers using their smartphones during business meetings to release (or approve) wire transfers and ACH transactions. The device gave them the ability to multi-task. So, what's the problem, you ask?

The Security Issue

Most organizations take the security of the computers used by their employees very seriously. Anti-fraud and virus protection software is loaded onto the machines and updated regularly. What's more, many organizations have guidelines for their staff as to how and when different programs can be used. And many organizations block some or all of the social media sites (like Facebook, LinkedIn and YouTube).

All this goes out the door when employees use their own personal devices for company business. Even if virus protection software was originally put on the device, many people don't regularly update it. Most regularly surf the Internet with their devices. And, some visit websites that might be prone to enabling malware attacks. All this flies in the face of what best-practice organizations have been doing to protect their technology and information from invasions from fraudsters.

Now, to be fair, virtually all employees who bring their own devices to work to use for business, think they are doing a good thing. They are certainly not looking to weaken the organization's defenses against fraudsters. This is such a new issue; the implications have not been analyzed or discussed much. And many employees are not aware there are issues.

The Corporate Stance

There are two basic ways to address this issue. To begin with, every organization needs to analyze the issue and have a corporate policy. Right now, only about one-quarter of all organizations have a policy (and we suspect most of those organizations are larger ones.).

The policy can take one of two thrusts:

1. Employees are asked not to use their personal devices for company business. In this case, the policy is mandatory and employees are not given any leeway.

2. Employees are permitted to use personal devices, but only after they bring them to IT and have the appropriate anti-virus software loaded onto the machine. They are also required to bring the devices back periodically to have the software updated.

Unfortunately, at this point, most organizations are silent on this issue. This is an issue that needs to be brought to management's attention. At that point, a task force comprised of IT folks and all interested/affected business users can make a recommendation on what the organization's BYOD policy should be.

Accounts payable should fight to be part of this task force. This is a critical issue for the accounts payable function. While many of the other business users on this task force will be concerned about their data integrity (and this is an important issue, not to be disparaged) accounts payable is concerned about a critical issue: the organization's money, its lifeblood.

The Future for BYOD

Clearly, these devices are not going away. If anything, they will become more prevalent as new uses are found for them. What's more, some are predicting a change in the way some companies handle the purchase of IT for their employees. Of course, many will stay the current course of providing employees with the hardware or devices they select. That presents problems for some employees who could conceivably end up carrying around two cell phones and two tablets. Such a scenario would not make their lives any easier.

Some see a move towards companies giving employees an "allowance" if they prefer to purchase their own devices rather than rely on those provided by the organization. For example, a company might give an employee who had a business need for a tablet and a smartphone, a $600 annual stipend toward the purchase of these devices and perhaps a $50 monthly allowance towards monthly charges. Employees who took this option would be on their own in the case of upgrades or problems. Employees who went with the company-recommended devices could rely on IT for help in case of upgrades or problems.

There is no simple answer to what's the best policy. This is a new and evolving issue and it will take some time to sort it out. What's more, as you can probably guess, there will be additional issues to address. You might even have thought of some of them while reading this article.

The Issue

The Bring Your Own Device (BYOD) issue raises concern because most individuals do not have the same level of security on these devices as their employers put on the computers used by employees for their day-to-day tasks. Even if the virus protections are strong when the devise is new, few regularly update them.

These devices are being used by some employees to access and respond to e-mail, access the ERP system to update company financial and accounting records and access bank balance reporting and payment systems. It's not only the organization's data that is at risk, it's also their bank accounts.

The Decision

Many organizations have yet to address this issue. That is a huge mistake. Every organization needs to examine the issue and decide how to handle this issue. Those who have addressed it typically decide on one of the following strategies:

- They forbid employees from using personal devices for any work associated with the organization;
- They allow employees to use personal devices for work associated with the organization, only after the employee has brought the device to IT so the appropriate security software can be loaded onto it;
- They give employees the choice of an allowance towards the purchase of a personal device or using one provided by the organization.

Those that choose the last strategy also make it clear to employees that if they take the allowance, the IT staff will not help them with any technical issues they might have. They are on their own with that. Clearly, the organizations that take this approach would prefer that employees took the devise they were offering. However, many employees complain about having to carry around two phones, a laptop and perhaps a tablet as well. So, the allowance approach is a compromise on that front.

Whatever the path an organization chooses, it needs to have a formal policy in place for all its employees.

Creating a BYOD Policy for Your Organization

Before deciding on a corporate wide policy, all affected parties should be consulted. This may seem obvious, but more often than not, policies are set by top management and/or HR. In this case, it is critical that IT be included in the discussion. It also might not be a bad idea to include someone who fully understands how electronic payment fraud is committed and what needs to be done to stop it.

Once the decision has been made as to which path the organization intends to take, the policy should be communicated to all employees. Don't overlook the importance of sharing the decision that employees should NOT use personal devices for company business. If this is the path your organization chooses, it needs to be clearly communicated.

Issues to be Covered

At a minimum, the policy should address the following:

- Whether personal devices can be used;
- If personal devices are allowed, what steps the employee must take before using the devise for company activities;
- How much, if anything, the company is willing to pay towards the purchase of the devise;
- How much, if anything, the company is willing to pay towards monthly charges;
- Instructions on whether the devise can be used for company business utilizing public open access internet connectivity (say in airports or local coffee shops);
- How frequently virus protection software should be updated;
- What to do if the device is lost or stolen;
- If the company paid for all or part of the device, what happens to it when the employee leaves the company;
- What happens to data that might be on the devise when the employee leaves the company (including company e-mail mailboxes);
- Any limitations as to which devices can be used to access which resources (for example, maybe the organization would prefer company bank accounts not be accessed with smartphones);

- Guidelines as to what an employee should do if he or she thinks their device has been compromised.

Other Considerations

In addition to policies for employees, every organization allowing the use of personal devices needs to put in place procedures to ensure the program runs smoothly. It will need to decide the following:

- Whether use of personal devices is monitored at the corporate level, the departmental level or both;
- Who will track that all devices are regularly updated with the latest security protocols;
- Who is responsible for updating policies and procedures for employees;
- Practices to ensure devices are retrieved (if that is the policy) when an employee leaves the company;
- Protocols for removing company data from devices owned by employees who leave the company;
- What, if any, periodic reporting should be done regarding number of devices, level of use etc.;
- Who will be responsible for reviewing departmental policies regarding use of personal devices to ensure that at a minimum they meet corporate guidelines.

This is a new and evolving area. The issues related to it are just starting to emerge. We fully expect this topic to not only develop more nuances but become one of those standard issues every organization addresses. However, we are probably a few years away from that.

Mary S. Schaeffer

Chapter 17 Controls to Prevent the
Bribing of Foreign Government Officials

Many readers probably know the Foreign Corrupt Practices Act (FCPA) prohibits bribing foreign government officials and they may wonder how this impacts the accounts payable function and why it is being covered in a work on internal controls in accounts payable.

After all, no one in accounts payable will be in a position to initiate a bribe of a foreign government official. And, this is most decidedly true. However, accounts payable is the last set of eyes to see a transaction before the money goes out the door; they are the last control for a company looking to conform to the law. Therefore, it is imperative that they review payments for potential violations. It is also why many experts now recommend that employees be given some training in this area.

In this section we'll take a look at:

- What's required by the Act
- Payments that are exempt from the Act
- Where and what to look for as potential bribes

Background

In mid-seventies, an SEC investigation found over 400 companies admitted to making questionable or illegal payments in excess of $300 million for the purpose of securing favorable action by foreign governments.

As you might imagine, many of these transactions did not cast a favorable light on the companies that made the payments and Americans in general. As a result, FCPA legislation was passed in 1977 and *all* US companies doing business outside US must be familiar with it.

In the last ten years or so, there have been several large cases where the organizations involved received a lot of bad press and paid large fines for violating this law. This has raised the profile of the issue.

Basics of FCPA

Simply put, FCPA prohibits corrupt payments to foreign officials for the purpose of gaining or keeping business. While it sounds simple enough, it is anything but. There are exceptions discussed later in this piece.

The Act is enforced by Department of Justice for criminal and civil enforcements and the SEC for civil enforcement with respect to issuers of securities.

What Constitutes a Violation?

When trying to determine if you have a potential violation, examine the following five factors.

- **Factor #1** Who does the act apply to? Any of the following individuals acting on behalf of the firm:

  - Individual
  - Firm
  - Officer
  - Director
  - Employee
  - Agent of the firm
  - Individuals or firms who order, authorize or assist someone else in violating the Act

- **Factor #2** Is there corrupt intent? Is the party involved trying to get the recipient to misuse his/her official position to direct business wrongly to your company or another. Note: To be guilty, you don't have to be successful!

- **Factor #3.** Examine the payment. Not only can't you pay, offer to pay or promise to pay, you can't authorize others to pay. And that payment can be money or anything else of value. This is where T&E can play a role.

- **Factor #4** Examine the recipient. This is where it can get really tricky. Payments (for FCPA purposes) should not be made to any of the following:

  - Foreign official
  - Officer, employee of
  - Foreign government
  - Public international organizations
  - Department or agency (of the above)
  - Any person acting in an official capacity
  - Foreign political party
  - Party official
  - Candidate for foreign political office

- **Factor #5** Does it meet the business purpose test? FCPA references "obtaining or retaining business." This is interpreted broadly and refers to both the awarding of new business as well as the renewal of existing business.

One Last Caveat

Do not try and find a way around the legislation. No payments may be made through third-party intermediaries. Simply put; if you know that a portion of the payment will be used for corrupt purposes, you cannot make it.

Please also be aware that as far as the SEC and DOJ are concerned with this legislation, knowing includes "conscious disregard and deliberate ignorance." Every organization affected by this legislation is expected to know and understand its requirements and ramifications and make sure their employees abide by it.

Exceptions

As mentioned earlier, there are a few exceptions to these rules. They include facilitating payments for routine government actions including:

- Obtaining permits, licenses or other official documents
- Processing government papers (e.g. visas, work orders)
- Providing police protection
- Mail pick-up and delivery
- Providing phone service, power and water supply
- Loading and unloading cargo
- Protecting perishable products
- Scheduling inspections associated with contract performance or transit of goods

Where to Look for Bribery Payments

Bribes are rarely put through on an invoice or check request marked Bribe. So, the savvy investigator has to look through payments from a rather-different angle. They have to be able to identify those payments that appear to be normal but are actually a bribe. They can take many forms but generally will appear as one of the following:

1. A typical invoice for payment
2. Consultants' invoices
3. On an employee's expense report

In this section we'll look at all three.

1. Typical invoices

Bribes are sometimes passed through as a typical invoice. It is the job of the person reviewing invoices to ferret these questionable payments out for further investigation. Here are a few of the issues that should raise a red flag with your processors:

1. Falsified invoices

2. Invoices where very little detail is offered

3. Invoices not showing services performed or goods ordered

4. Invoices for infrequent, high-unit price sales to government agencies

5. Use of non-standard invoice forms

6. Requests for cash payments (this should set off a mega red flag)

7. Agents requiring cash payments

8. High management fees

9. High entertainment fees (may be on T&E)

10. Expensive gifts (may be on T&E)

11. Checks made out to cash or "bearer"

12. Indirect payments (sometimes bribes are disguised using third parties)

13. Wire transfers with scanty backup

14. Wire transfers without the identity of the recipient

15. Requests for large, unsubstantiated up-front payments

16. Payments for "office overhead"

17. Requests for campaign contributions to foreign party candidates not to be disclosed

18. Unusual payment patterns, either round amounts or payments made on weekends or holidays

19. Vague contracts

20. Unnecessary third-party performing services

21. Close connections or family member of senior officials of government or ruling party (although the staff in accounts payable is unlikely to be able to determine this)

As you can see, there are a lot of ways a savvy employee can disguise a bribe.

2. Consultants' Invoices

Distinguishing between when you have a legitimate consultant's invoice and when you have an invoice that is really a request for a payment that is a bribe is not an easy task. Here are a few signs that you might be dealing with a payment that is a bribe and not a normal consultant fee for services.

1. The consultant refuses to sign a representation indicating he/she is in compliance with FCPA requirements
2. The consultant refuses to disclose complete ownership of their organization
3. The consultant resides outside the country where services were rendered
4. There is a high commission without a corresponding high level of service

When reviewing consultant invoices, the processor should:

1. Look for a written, signed detailed agreement
2. Review the disbursement records for fees described as "consulting" or sub-contracting
3. Make sure there is detailed backup for payments

3. Travel and Entertainment Expense Reports and FCPA Risk Management

As you may know the Foreign Corrupt Practices Act (FCPA) prohibits the bribing of foreign government officials. These bribes can take many forms and are not necessarily the payment of hard cash. One area that is often overlooked when it comes to bribery is the organization's travel and entertainment policy (T&E). Let's take a look at what the reviewer of expense reports should look for and what they should do if they suspect a bribe.

What Should You Look for

For starters, review T&E policy and make sure it contains FCPA compliance language as well as details of what should not be done. Educating traveling employees is an important first step. Educating the staff who reviews the expense reports is also an essential component, for they are the last set of eyes to look at a payment before it goes out the door. Another words, they are your last opportunity to prevent an infraction of the law that could land your organization in hot water with the Department of Justice and/or the SEC.

When reviewing expense reports of employees, look for the following words:

- Bribe
- Kickback
- Payoff
- Gift
- Present
- Entertainment

If you find any, further investigation is warranted. While you would hope that your employees would not include words like bribe or kickback on an expense report, it is not safe to assume none will.

When reviewing expense reports, be suspicious of round sum receipts. The nature of business travel is such that it normally does not result in receipts for round numbers. While consultant fees are often round amounts, they are not typically handled through the expense reimbursement process – nor should they be.

Clearly, invoices should not be paid through the expense reimbursement process. If any are submitted in this manner, they should immediately be removed for further scrutiny.

Identify reimbursement made to government agencies or officials for visits. Then verify the reasonableness of reimbursement amount as well as the appropriateness of the transaction.

This is something the reviewer may need help with. It may be necessary to contact the submitter's superiors to ascertain whether the expense is reasonable and not bribery.

What Should You Do if You Suspect Bribery Is Involved

First, realize that many of the items identified as suspicious will turn out to be false positives. This does not mean they should be disregarded. All should be investigated further. The investigation should not initially include the employee who submitted the expense.

The reviewer should bring the questionable expense to the attention of their manager and then the controller. At that point, an expert in this issue should be called in for further consultation. If you are an organization with lots of international business, it is likely you have an attorney on staff responsible for reviewing these issues. At some point, during this investigation, when management feels it appropriate, the employee who submitted the expense will be questioned about it.

What This Means for Accounts Payable

For starters, at all affected companies, the staff should understand what is expected by FCPA. This is not intuitive or something that is normally part of training for the accounts payable function. This means that there should be some special training for the accounts payable staff. There should be written procedures which can be included in the policy and procedures manual.

The staff should also be alerted to the fact that if they find a possible FCPA violation, it should be brought to management's attention for handling. This needs to be addressed at a higher level. The staff should be warned to expect many false positives. You will find quite a few questionable payments that upon further investigation will turn out to be perfectly legitimate transactions.

Before you completely dismiss this issue, be aware that if a bribe can slip through, the likelihood of another improper payment making it out the door is high. The controls you put in place to stop a bribe could end up doing double duty stopping other inappropriate payments.

Chapter 18: Other Issues That Present Control Concerns

Before we close, we want to address a few other internal control issues that didn't seem to fit in any of the other chapters. The issue of internal controls when it comes to accounts payable covers a wide variety of issues. Miss one and you have a chance of weakening your entire system of controls. That's why, in this section we pick up the few odd topics that did not readily fit under the other categories addressed so far.

In this section we'll look at controls (or lack of controls) related to:

- The Super User and his or her impact on the control function
- Tactics needed to protect the organization when employees leave (regardless of who instigated the separation)
- The problems created by the sharing of P-cards
- The problems created by the sharing of passwords
- The problems management overrides create and what to do when you must allow a management override
- Dumpster diving and confidential information
- Control issues with petty cash boxes
- How complaints might signify a internal control breakdown and what to look for

The Super User

The Super User, the Semi-Super User and Their Impact on Internal Controls

In the computer world, the super user is typically the system administrator, the person with access to everything. He or she is the person who manages the system and makes sure everyone has what they need. They don't get involved with the nitty-gritty unless there is a problem. Then they are there to help. While there is a great deal of logic to having such a person, it can lead to internal control issues.

The Issue

The real concern, at least for the accounts payable function, comes from the semi-super users, those individuals who have access to everything under the accounting umbrella. This might be any one of the following:

- The professional who oversees the accounting and finance departments technology issues

- The accounts payable manager who wants to be able to train new employees and/or fill in when someone is unexpectedly absent

- The controller/CFO/VP of finance who believes they need this or should have this access due to their level within the organization

The Problem

By having this far-reaching system access—no matter how worthy the reasons might seem—the segregation of duties logic for the organization is compromised. And, that weakens the system and introduces risk into the process. When you talk about risk in the process in accounts payable, the payment function (and hence the bottom line) is negatively impacted.

By having even one employee with access to the entire procure-to-pay chain, the organization has taken on a risk it shouldn't have. Trusted employees have been known to turn out to be not completely upright. What's more, they've also been tricked out of their passwords by the unscrupulous.

The final consideration in this regard relates the hijacking of computers. While this won't happen often, once is too much. Should a computer be hijacked (see more about this in the electronic payment fraud section), the crooks could end up with complete access to your computer system. If you have any sort of sensitive data, like credit card information etc., you could have additional problems.

The Solution

The answer here is fairly obvious. There should be no super or semi-super users when it comes to the procure-to-pay chain. Yes, some of the ease of operation that might be achieved by having a super user is eliminated. But so is the risk that the super user decides to take advantage of this status. The best control, and the one everyone should rely on, is having complete segregation of duties, without any exceptions.

When Employees Leave the Organization

This is an area that is often overlooked entirely. It is important to remember that these steps apply regardless of the reason the employee separates from the organization. The steps should be the same when a much-respected employee leaves for a new higher level position as when an employee is terminated for cause. When the employee leaves the company, he or she still has access to a number of things, unless steps are taken to cut those ties. Among other things, these can include:

- Access to the computer system, if it has not been terminated as discussed above

- Access to credit card sales, if the credit card has not been returned and canceled with the bank

- Access to potential expense reimbursement requests, if the employee has not been inactivated in the master vendor file

- Access to email, unless the account has been blocked or all messages automatically forwarded to a current employee

- The ability to sign a check, release a wire transfer, initiate or release an ACH payment on behalf of the organization
- Access to the building, if the key and/or employee identification card have not been returned

The Ideal Process

Whether HR's plate is already overflowing or not, they are the central repository for information about all employees. They are also typically involved with all employee separations, whether pleasant or remarkably unpleasant. This means that they are in the best position to notify everyone who needs to know about an employee departure.

As it relates to accounts payable, this means some departing employees have the access to do real financial harm to the organization, unless appropriate and timely action is taken. Therefore, it is critical that accounts payable be notified so they can inform the bank and terminate the financial privileges of the departing employee.

Avoiding the Card Problem Completely

Occasionally, when it comes to cards (p-cards, travel cards, fuel cards etc.), companies are under the false impression that they can simply get the card back and take no further action. This would work if everyone were honorable. However, an employee who wants to play games can simply note the card number, expiration date and three or four digit code.

Then, they can shop online using your credit card numbers to their hearts content.

Can you get your money back? Maybe – but you'll have to get it from the employee and that won't happen without a lot of stress and aggravation. A must better approach is to simply cancel the card with the bank and not have the problem in the first place.

When HR Doesn't Notify AP

Sometimes, no matter how hard the AP staff tries, they cannot get on HR's radar with regard to departing employees. In those cases, AP needs to approach the problem from a different angle. There are some steps that can be taken to work around the issue. Some best practice organizations, concerned about tight internal controls, perform some of these tasks in addition to the best practices discussed above to ensure they are well protected.

The additional procedures include:

- Periodically getting a list of inactive card-holders from the financial institution issuing the cards and investigating whether those on the list have left the organization or are simply not using their cards

- Periodically getting a list of active employees and running it against the list of cardholders and authorized signers to identify employees who have left

- Periodically running a report showing which employees have access to accounts payable functionalities and closing those that should not be in place

Occasionally, management will be lulled into a false sense of security thinking that a departing employee was happy with the company and thus not taking proper steps. Don't fall into that trap. Don't underestimate the importance of taking care of what some think of as loose ends. They are anything but that.

The IT Component

As the business world becomes more dependent on technology, there are more issues to consider. By notifying IT at the same time, the accounts payable function is protected, assuming IT cuts the associated system access.

This protects the organization from an employee trying to wreak havoc with your data. And, in the off-chance the employee is hired back by the company at a later date, it helps prevent potential segregation of duties issues at a later date.

As more and more employees use their personal devices (smartphones, tablets and laptops), there is also the issue of company data on these devices. Some organizations automatically wipe their data from the devices while others ignore the issues completely, perhaps not even aware that the employee has been using a personal device. This issue must be addressed and confidential data and access should be removed.

Sharing P-cards

Occasionally, organizations let several employees share one card rather than issue them to those who might only occasionally need them,. This penny-wise-pound-foolish approach is just that—foolish. And when you look at it from an internal controls standpoint sharing cards stands out as a phenomenally bad idea.

If you think sharing cards wouldn't happen in your organization, consider whether any departments share a card because no one purchases enough to warrant their own—or so the reasoning goes. Please note: This is different than using ghost cards where the vendor has one card for the entire organization and that card is used for purchases with that vendor alone. In those cases the vendor should be responsible for tracking who made what purchase.

The reason why a card should not be shared is simple. With several users the organization loses the single point of accountability and increases the possibility for fraud. Since no one can tell who made the charge, it's hard to assign responsibility.

Even if fraud isn't the issue, people can be quite absentminded. By the time the bill comes in the purchaser will have completely forgotten that they even used the card. Of course, in these situations the receipt is bound to be long gone.

The use of a single card for multiple employees also leaves open the issue of who is responsible for seeing that all of the charges are properly allocated. And, of course, if there is a mistake in an allocation there could be finger pointing when it comes to resolution. It doesn't take much thought to begin to identify the problems that could arise—and they far outweigh the small benefit of not issuing a few extra cards. What first appeared as a obvious winner of an idea to save a few dollars may turn out to be a really big loser.

Sharing Passwords

Again virtually all our readers are aware that the sharing of passwords is not a good thing, in fact it is on the list of worst practices. Yet, when faced with the situation of the vacation of an employee who is the only one handling a particular task, a few might be tempted to have the employees simply share the vacationing employee's password.

Resist the Temptation

That is a very bad practice and muddies audit trails. What's more, even after the vacationing employee has returned, there is no guaranteeing the employee who had temporary rights to the password will forget it. Some think that by having the vacationing employee change their password upon their return, they have effectively handled the problem. This is not a 100% safeguard. If there is a fraud while the employee is on vacation that can be traced back to the ID used during that time period, you have no proof as to who committed the transaction.

Best practice advice in this situation is to set up the employee handling the tasks temporarily with his/her own password and rescind those privileges when the vacationing employee returns.

Another Password Control Issue:
Sticky Notes on The Side of a Computer

And speaking of passwords, here's another problem that creeps into the accounts payable process from time to time. Like most people, professionals handling the accounts payable function have too many passwords to remember. A few, take the short cut of writing them down and posting them on a sticky note on the side of the computer.

While this might make it a little easier for them to log into the variety of systems they have to access in the course of a day, it makes it easy for anyone coming through the department to steal their passwords. This includes all sorts of unknown personnel who might be on the premises after hours. The simple action when it comes to password on sticky notes on the side of the computer is don't have them. Whether they are passwords to log into the ERP system or passwords to log into online banking, they are a bad practice.

Managers who notice such notes should immediately require their staff to remove them, explaining the risk. If the employee seems reluctant, remind the person that should a fraud be perpetrated using information obtained in this manner, it will look as though the employee is the guilty party.

Management Overrides

One method used by disingenuous employees to hide questionable activity is the management override. This helps cover their tracks, usually relating to a fraud, elsewhere within the business. Now, let's be clear. We are not saying that all management overrides are meant to hide fraud. Nothing could be farther from the truth.

Management overrides are meant to address legitimate problems. They may be caused by errors in data entry, data that arrives after the final cut-off date or other justifiable issues. Unfortunately, over the years, unscrupulous employees also figured out they could be used to cover questionable transactions, make financial statements look better than they actually were or hide issues they prefer not be disclosed.

For this reason they are considered the weak link in the financial statement process and should be avoided at all costs. A much better approach, at least from an internal control standpoint, is for the necessary transactions to be entered through normal channels, negating the need for the management override.

Should an override be absolutely required for whatever reason, additional approvals should be required. It should not be possible for one person to put the override through. At a minimum, one should enter it while a second person approves or releases it.

Dumpster Diving and Confidential Information

Accounts payable can be a trove of valuable information, data that many crooks would pay dearly for. It is truly worth its weight in gold. Therefore before throwing anything in the trash, an evaluation should be made as to whether the data should be shredded or can be thrown in the normal trash.

Lists of bank accounts, lists of authorized signers, credit card information, banking data etc. should all be shredded as should unused paper checks that will not be used. As a matter of course, the rule of thumb when it comes to shredding should be: when in doubt, shred.

Shred anything containing a bank account number or other sensitive information

Petty Cash

It will probably come as no surprise to those reading this to learn that a petty cash box is not a recommended practice for any organization interested in strong internal controls. Yet, despite acknowledging this fact, about 25% of all organizations admit to having one. Given this reality, we thought it appropriate to include a look at this function. It provides a treasure trove of opportunities for internal control disasters.

The Recommended Approach

If the company insists on a petty cash box, and in some circumstances corporate culture or industry peculiarities dictate one, limit its use as much as possible. This can be done by placing a low-dollar threshold for transactions handled through the petty cash box. The threshold can be lowered over time.

Here are some tactics you can take to keep the petty cash function in check.

1) Have a detailed written policy delineating the use of the box. Specifically, spell out what can be reimbursed from the box.

2) Never reimburse an item that should be put through on an expense report. It will be next to impossible to find duplicate submissions.

3) Limit the access to the box to one or two individuals. Allowing too many people access is a guarantee to losing control.

4) Keep a log of who goes into the box, the beginning balance, all withdrawals and the ending balance. Ideally two individuals should verify these items and initial the log, each time an entry is made.

5) Internal audit should perform unscheduled audits of the box. (See more on surprise audits further in this piece.).

6) Limit the hours when the employees can request reimbursement and the box is open. Don't reimburse employees whenever they show up (unless of course it is a true emergency). If possible, open the box only once a week to reimburse employees.

7) When the box is not open for reimbursement, it should be locked away in a secure location.

8) Whenever a reimbursement is requested, look for other ways to handle the charge. Even if the employee is paid from the box, point out ways the matter could be addressed in the future without resorting to petty cash.

9) Never, under any circumstances, take an IOU in the petty cash box.

10) Never, reimburse an employee who does not have proper documentation and authorization for the expense.

11) Do not reimburse items through the petty cash box that are not allowed by the organization's expense reimbursement policy.

12) Replenish the box on a timely basis. Don't allow the box to run too low on cash.

13) Set stringent checks on who can take money in and out of the box. With several hands in the pot, it can get ugly if money is missing.

14) Publish a schedule of when the box will be open, along with the requirements for reimbursement, and share it with all employees likely to use the box.

15) Periodically, review the expenses reimbursed from the box and look for alternative ways to pay for those expenses.

16) Keep only a small amount of cash in the box. Otherwise you could have other problems.

Petty Cash Awful Practices

Don't think I am making the stuff up in this section. I have seen all these practices in play and I'm betting most reading this have as well.

- Cashing personal checks in the box.

- Accepting post-dated personal checks in the box.

- Accepting an IOU from an employee for cash in the box.

- Reimbursing employees for expenditures that should have been put on an expense report.

- Borrowing by the petty cash administrator without putting an IOU in the box.

- Keeping other valuables in the petty cash box.

Surprise Audits

From time to time, internal audit or other accounting manager should perform a spot check on the petty cash box and the records. These surprise audits should verify that:

- Vouchers are signed with supporting documentation attached.

- The cash is regularly counted and the balance agreed to the petty cash records.

- The staff is not borrowing from petty cash.

- None of the other poor practices delineated above are in place.

If you are in a business that gets paid with cash, any cash should be kept separately in an income cash box and not mixed with petty cash. While it might be tempting to reimburse the petty cash box from your cash register, resist the temptation

While it might not be the best use of the accounts payable department's time and resources, if management decrees that there should be a petty cash box, accounts payable will have to run it. Use the practices discussed above to help ensure the controls are tight and no problems arise due to petty cash issues.

Complaints

Complaints are a part of doing business, a necessary evil. They have to be dealt with, they are often unreasonable and they really don't add value to your bottom line. Yet, they shouldn't be completely dismissed out of hand as they may be red flag of an internal control problem. Let's take a look at two such instances.

- Vendor complaints. Do you investigate vendor complaints thoroughly, especially the ones that sound outlandish? Sometimes the complaints not only are legitimate they are a result of an employee playing games for their own enrichment. Of course, the perpetration of the fraud could be by the vendor so don't jump to conclusions right away.

- Customer complaints. Just like the grievances of your vendors, your customers may have legitimate gripes caused by an ongoing fraud being committed by one of your employees. So, follow up and investigate closely.

And, as with the vendor issues, it could be the customer trying to pull the wool over your eyes.

This section contained an odd assortment of issues that did not fit in under the other topics discussed in this work. Don't think that means they were an afterthought or not important. Quite the opposite is true. Upon reflection of the topics covered it was recognized these had not been addressed but were important to establishing strong controls in the procure-to-pay function. Hence they were grouped together here.

Chapter 19 Policy and Procedures Manual: Tying It All Together

Because many accounts payable departments have grown gradually or evolved as part of the accounting department, few have a written game plan. Instead, procedures are developed on an as-needed basis, in kind of a hodgepodge manner. Moreover, much of the knowledge about how things work and where information is located often resides with specific individuals. If those individuals get sick or accept another job, the company is left in a lurch. In this section, we discuss:

- The importance of having a policy and procedures manual
- The manual from a control standpoint
- The manual as an ongoing project

Why a Policy and Procedures Manual Is Needed

Every accounts payable department should have a procedures manual, to serve not only as a guide in case of an emergency, but also to provide managers with the necessary documentation to demonstrate to management the capabilities of the staff and the work they are handling. Without such a document, few understand the scope of information that is needed to run a successful department. This is especially important for those organizations subject to the strictures of the Sarbanes-Oxley Act.

The procedures manual can also be used to determine whether any processes can be eliminated. Needless to say, this document will not be the most interesting book ever written, but it is essential. As an added benefit, it will make the auditors happy. The manual should not only be prepared by those who are actually doing the day-to-day tasks, but it should also be updated regularly. Some choose to do this anytime a process is amended or added, whereas others do it annually. It is imperative that this be done. You'd be surprised to discover just how much processes change over the course of a year.

There is one other reason to have this manual and insist that everyone follow it. Left to their own devices, processors in accounts payable will gradually develop their own procedures. Without a careful and periodic review, each person will end up handling transactions differently. There is a word for this, and it is *chaos*. If one processor has an idea for an improved way of doing a particular task, the suggestion should be raised with the manager. If it is determined that the suggestion is superior to the methodology in use, everyone should change how they handle that particular task, and the policy and procedures manual should be updated to reflect this change.

Now, if this seems to be a cumbersome and costly task, think again. Thanks to the Internet, many companies now post their manuals on their corporate intranet site. This makes it available to anyone who may need to check it. It also makes updating a snap, and there are no costly printing charges each time the manual is updated. Finally, putting all the latest changes on the intranet removes that old chestnut of an excuse: "nobody told me." E-mail alerts can be sent to everyone who is affected each time the policy is updated.

If your accounts payable department does not have a policy and procedures manual, the staff should bite the bullet and prepare one. If topics are divided among the staff and each one writes a chapter or two, the work will not seem overly burdensome. If you need some samples, do a search on the Internet.

You'll come up with numerous samples that you can modify to fit your own procedures. One word of caution regarding those Internet policies, however: Most are written by universities. If you are in a manufacturing environment, you may have to add several sections. Still, having something to start with is a big help.

Finally, once the manual is completed, especially if it includes your T&E procedures, all affected parties should be notified that they will be expected to conform to the policies. Expect a certain amount of complaining. To make sure the policy is enforced, the first notice to the staff should come from a high-level executive (e.g., the controller or the CFO). Some companies put a short note from this executive on the front page of the policy so everyone understands that they will be expected to adhere to it. This is especially important when it comes to issues like T&E, Rush checks, and not returning checks to requisitioners.

The Policy and Procedures Manual from a Control Standpoint

Like the semiannual visit to the dentist, most professionals know they should have a policy and procedures manual, but only a small percentage actually do. Even in those organizations that finally do get one put together, it is rarely updated. While Sarbanes-Oxley doesn't actually mandate a policy and procedures manual for accounts payable, it's hard to visualize many situations where one would be considered in compliance without one.

If you've flowcharted your processes, a good portion of the work producing the manual has been completed. The task at hand is converting that diagram into words, keeping it updated, and making sure it reflects what actually goes on in the department.

What sometimes happens, with both the manual and the flowchart, is that over time, processes drift from the documented policy to something else. Unfortunately, that something else often introduces weaknesses and control points into the process. Sometimes, in an effort to speed up the work, steps are omitted from the process or the segregation of duties requirements are voided.

The policy and procedures manual should be shared with all affected parties. This means that, for example, purchasing should have input into and be given the final version of all sections that affect it. It is meaningless to write a policy that will require a three-day turnaround time of invoices if interoffice mail is used and it is slow. Similarly, if the purchasing manager is required to approve all invoices and he travels extensively, a lengthy approval time will be required unless electronic mechanisms are used or the board authorization for spending approvals can be further delegated.

Many organizations now post their accounts payable policy and procedures manual on their company intranet sites. This makes the information available to anyone who needs it, makes updating it relatively easy, and keeps it on the forefront of everyone's mind. It also makes it easy to refer people with questions to the manual rather than have accounts payable answer every question. From a control standpoint, this is recommended.

It forces everyone to use the same source document for procedures rather than relying on one individual's memory, which may or may not be accurate. Readers should be aware that having a policy and procedures manual can come back to haunt them if the staff does not adhere to it. By posting it on the intranet, or making it readily available using some other mechanism, the department is announcing its requirements. It makes it relatively easy to uncover situations where the policy is not adhered to by the accounts payable staff.

The Policy and Procedures Manual: An Ongoing Project

Very little in life remains static, and accounts payable is no exception. Even if you think you have policies and procedures exactly the way you like them, circumstances outside the control of the department may force a change. A move to a new accounting system, starting to use electronic payment alternatives, a demand by a key supplier, a physical move by a group within the organization, a new CFO, or any one of a thousand other things can cause the department to need to implement change.

The very best manuals are updated every time a change to the procedures is made. This is one of the benefits of posting the manual online instead of printing hard copies. Of course this is probably not realistic in most organizations. At least once a year the manual should be reviewed and updated. This is also a good time to ensure that the procedures detailed in the manual are actually being followed in the department. You will be surprised to find how often they are not.

Including a Flowchart Is Not a Bad Idea

Most experts recommend that the department's operations be flowcharted as part of the Sarbanes-Oxley compliance process. This is a good idea even without the Act. It forces the discipline of reviewing the ongoing process and documenting it. This flowchart should not be completed in a vacuum. It needs to accurately represent the work flow of the department, not what the manager or executives would like the work flow to look like.

It should be completed with input from the individuals who do the work. When it is completed, someone should verify that what's in the chart is how the work actually is done. This is a great opportunity for the manager who believes some of the group's processes are more cumbersome than they need to be. Once the chart is completed, it can be reviewed for two reasons:

1. To ensure that the appropriate controls are in place

2. To determine whether there are any processes on the chart that are unnecessary

This last analysis is key to getting rid of non-value-added steps. There is a good reason for eliminating these extraneous steps. They can actually weaken controls. Here's an example: In some organizations all hand-signed checks must be reviewed by an assistant treasurer before they are mailed. At the company in question, the checks often sit on this individual's desk for two or three days before he or she releases them. While ostentatiously this is a review process, the real reason for the review is that this is how the assistant treasurer monitors what other departments are spending--something that is none of his professional business.

If the appropriate up-front controls are in place, this review adds nothing but time and additional risk (someone could take the checks from his frequently unoccupied office) to the process. By including this step in the process, it highlights the inefficiency. To further highlight the process, include estimated time frames with each step. This will become useful in those situations where management is demanding (often rightly so) that the procure-to-pay cycle be accelerated. Simply take out the flowchart, with the time frames noted, and ask where the time should be cut from the process.

One of the biggest bottlenecks in many organizations is the invoice-approval process. It is not unusual to see two thirds or more of the cycle time being allotted to getting the invoice approved. This is especially true if electronic invoicing, imaging, and work flow are not being used. The flowchart will highlight these inefficiencies. Accounts payable professionals can use this chart to back their recommendations for imaging, work flow, and/or electronic invoicing.

Mary S. Schaeffer

Glossary

ACFE – Association of Certified Fraud Examiners

ACH – Automated Clearing House

ACH credit – An electronic payment initiated by the payor

ACH debit – An electronic payment initiated by the payee

B-Notice - An annual IRS notification to payers, that IRS Forms 1099 have been filed with either missing or incorrect name/TIN combinations.

BYOD – Bring Your Own Device, generally refers to smartphones and tablets, but a few include laptops in the term.

DOJ – Department of Justice

Duplicate Payment – The unintentional second payment of an invoice. One type of erroneous payment and unfortunately, rarely returned by the vendor unless the customer or its audit firm discover the over payment.

e-Invoice – An electronic invoice either provided through an automated approach or as simple attachment to an e-mail. Some do not consider files attached to e-mail as true electronic invoices.

FCPA – Foreign Corrupt Practices Act

Form 1099 – The Form 1099 is used to report different types of taxable income; the most common for the accounts payable groups being Form 1099MISC. This is used to report income paid to independent contractors.

IFO – Institute of Financial Operations

Internal Controls - The group of policies and procedures implemented within the organization to prevent intentional or unintentional misuse of funds for unauthorized purposes.

MCC - Merchant Category Code

NACHA - National Automated Clearing House Association

OFAC – Office of Foreign Assets Control

P-card – Sometimes referred to as corporate procurement card or purchasing card.

Packing slip – Sometimes referred to as receiving documents, delineates exactly what was delivered in a particular shipment. Used in the three-way match.

PO – Purchase Order

Receiving documents – See packing slip.

S-Ox – Sarbanes Oxley Act

SEC – Securities and Exchange Commission

Segregation of Duties – With regards to accounts payable, it is the division of work so that one person does not perform more than one leg of the procure-to-pay function. It is one of the foundation principles of strong internal controls.

Three-way Match – Comparison of invoice with purchase order and receiving documents before payment is made. If there is a discrepancy, some investigation is required to eliminate the discrepancy before payment is made.

T&E – Travel and Entertainment

UCC – Uniform Commercial Code

W-9 – Its full name is Request for Taxpayer Identification Number and Certification and it is provided to customers who need to verify certain tax reporting information.

Index

Book Excerpts

Mary S. Schaeffer

Excerpt from:
101 Best Practices for Accounts Payable

Issue: Who Has Access to the Master Vendor File

While it is definitely easier for the staff processing invoices for payment if they can add vendors to the master vendor file whenever they get an invoice from a new vendor that practice is an invitation to trouble. Unfortunately, that's how a number of organizations handle information into the master vendor file. This means giving access to the master vendor file to a large number of individuals. This is a terrible idea. It completely disregards the best practice concept inherent in all accounting functions of having appropriate segregation of duties.

Best Practice: Access to the master vendor file, for anything but information lookup, should be severely limited. Only a few people should be able to enter information, be it for setup or to make changes. The employees with this access should not perform any other tasks in the procure-to-pay function making it more difficult for someone to defraud the organization. What's more, when they go on vacation, their passwords and access should not be given to someone else. This will simply muddy the audit trail should there be a problem down the line. A better approach is to set the back-up person up with their own user ID and password and then deactivate those when the person with primary responsibility for the task returns. This is less of a problem in large organizations where there will be several people working on the master vendor file.

Almost Best Practice: This is a black and white issue so there really is no almost best practice. In many organizations there is one or two people with access to the entire accounts payable function. Typically this is the manager, director or perhaps the Controller. While this is not a good idea, it does solve the problem of an unexpected absence, assuming the person with the broad access is willing to dive in and handle the task. Really, though, unlimited access is not a good idea.

Pointer for Accounts Payable: While limiting access for the purposes of adding new vendors or updating information on existing vendors can seem to make the accounts payable function run less smoothly, it is imperative from an internal control standpoint. Sometimes what is easier for accounts payable is not necessarily good for the organization as a whole and this is one of those instances.

Worst Practices:

- Letting each processor update information about their own vendors
- Letting each processor add vendors whenever it seems necessary

Excerpt from:
Fundamentals of Accounts Payable

Weeding out Duplicate Invoices

It would be nice if vendors would send one invoice and then wait for their payment. However, that doesn't always happen. When the payment isn't received by the due date, most vendors will send a second invoice. These are often not marked as a duplicate invoice or a copy of an invoice. It then falls to the accounts payable department to identify these unwanted seconds.

The Problem Gets Worse

Duplicate invoices have always been a problem. In the past they were typically sent only in the case of a late payment. That is now changing. Some vendors now send two invoices and this is creating massive headaches for the accounts payable staff who receive them.

There is an emerging problem of vendors emailing (or faxing) invoices and then for good measure because they want to make sure the invoice arrives, also mailing it as well. Whether the rationale for submitting the second invoice is devious or honest is irrelevant. It still means more work for accounts payable. That's why you need top-notch practices to identify these problematic second invoices.

The Game Plan

To deal with this issue, employing the following tactics will help identify and eliminate the duplicate invoices:

1. Identify those vendors sending by postal mail and e-mail and ask them to stop sending one of the ways. Occasionally, just asking vendors to stop sending multiple invoices solves the problem. However, many don't for a variety of reasons. Hence, it is critical to

know who's doing this and utilize extra checking routines on these vendors.

2. Centralize the receipt of invoices. This ensures accounts payable knows of all invoices as early in the cycle as possible. It also makes it less likely that a duplicate will slip through.

3. Insist that the accounts payable staff processing invoices uses standardized routines and rigid coding standards. This means that everyone who processes invoices uses exactly the same procedures. It also means setting up a coding standard for everyone to use when entering data so all data is entered the same, regardless of who enters the information. This step is critical. If you don't employ this step it is likely that duplicates will slip through.

4. Strong internal controls from the moment the invoice arrives in your office until the payment leaves are also an important component in any approach to eliminate duplicate invoices. This should apply not only to invoices sent through the postal mail, but also electronic invoices, as well.

5. Create an Always-Check-Thoroughly (ACT) list of vendors who routinely submit duplicate invoices. This will include not only those who submit through multiple channels but also those who are likely to send duplicates for other reasons.

6. Don't overlook the importance of staff training. When employees are first hired they should be trained by the most knowledgeable person available for the task. Periodically review their work to determine if additional training might be warranted. And, anytime a new process or procedure is introduced make sure everyone who might need it is given a thorough explanation of how the new process will work. Don't assume they will all figure it out. Also, update your policy and procedures manual with the new procedures so any employee who has questions can check on his or her own.

7. Don't overlook the benefits afforded by technology. With invoice automation, the task of identifying duplicates is a simple. Computers do an excellent job identifying duplicate invoices.

When all is said and done, sometimes despite the very best efforts of the accounts payable staff, a few duplicates do slip through and get paid. Unfortunately, rarely are those second payments returned by the vendors who received them unless some nudged by the vendor or its representatives. That's why a payment audit is highly recommended as a last step to identify those cases where an extra payment was made. Payment audits should be part of every best-practice accounts payable function.

To ensure that the payment auditors find as little as possible, implement as many of the steps described above as you can.

About Mary S. Schaeffer

Mary S. Schaeffer, a nationally recognized accounts payable expert, is the author of 18 business books, a monthly newsletter and a free bi-weekly e-zine, as well as several CPE courses for CPAs. She worked with the IFO to create the Innovating AP certificate program. She runs AP Now, a boutique publishing and consulting firm focused on accounts payable issues. Before turning to writing and consulting she worked in the corporate world as an Assistant Treasurer for the Equitable Life Assurance Society, a Financial Risk Manager for O&Y and a Corporate Cash Manager for Continental Grain. A frequent and popular speaker at industry, live and online events, she has an MBA in Finance and a BS in Mathematics.

About AP Now

AP Now is the leading source of accounts payable information for the business and finance community. It offers a host of products and services designed to advance your department, your company, and your career including:

- E-AP News bi-weekly ezine (free)
- Accounts Payable Now & Tomorrow Newsletter (monthly fee-based publication delivered by e-mail)
- Webinars/teleconferences
- Seminars – Accounts Payable and 1099
- CDs
- Books
- Consulting services (both corporate and vendor-related)
- Customized Training (including FCPA)
- Duplicate Payment Resource Center (complimentary)

www.ingramcontent.com/pod-product-compliance
Lightning Source LLC
Chambersburg PA
CBHW070717220326
41598CB00024BA/3197